THE OBJECT OF ROTARY

The object of Rotary is to encourage and foster the ideal of service as a basis of worthy enterprise and in particular to encourage and foster:

FIRST: The development of acquaintance as an opportunity for service.

SECOND: High ethical standards in business and professions, the recognition of the worthiness of all useful occupations, and the dignifying by each Rotarian of his occupation as an opportunity to serve society.

THIRD: The application of the ideal of service by every Rotarian to his personal, business and community life.

FOURTH; The advancement of international understanding, goodwill, and peace through a world fellowship of business and professional persons united in the ideal of service.

Rotarians Make A Difference!

"Rotarians Make A Difference"

First Edition:
September, 1999

Printed by: Dallas Offset, Dallas, Texas
Cover Design: Steve Cochran/Dallas/**C** CREATIVE

Acknowledgment

Several months ago, when the thought of writing a book on Rotary was just a "figment of my imagination", I realized full well that it could never be done without a lot of help from "my Rotary friends." (After all, what are friends for?)

Now that it has been done, I realize how right I was. I want to particularly thank those Rotarians who really made it possible. My sincere thanks to Rotary District Governor Bill Frew, Rotarians Charles D. McAdams, Mark Healy, and Pete Snider for their advice and counsel, as well as the 35 Rotarians who contributed the stories and vignettes. Each of them are truly dedicated Rotarians.

And my very special thanks to Rose, my wife of 51 years, for her understanding, consideration and support, before and during my 40 years in Rotary, and particularly during these last few months of "burning the midnight oil."

THANK YOU!

Preface

It was during the summer of 1997. I had been invited to attend the RYLA (Rotary Youth Leadership Award) conference at the YMCA camp in Estes Park, Colorado. More than 200 young high school students from Colorado and Wyoming were attending this annual leadership camp.

One morning a woman stopped me to ask directions; apparently she noticed my T-shirt, and pointing to the Rotary emblem, said "What's that?" I almost wanted to say, "Do you have a minute or an hour?" The simplest answer was that Rotary was an international service organization, and I added "with over a million members, in almost 30,000 clubs in over 160 nations throughout the world."

What is Rotary? To me, it's somewhat surprising that after 94 years of Rotary's existence, there are so many people who really don't know what Rotary is and what it does!

Rotary is.....SERVICE! People who truly care....for their community, their country and the world.

Occasionally, I'll comment to another Rotarian that "I've been in Rotary for 40 years...the first 20, I was a member of a Rotary Club and the last 20, I've become a Rotarian." Most of them understand what I am really saying. I joined the Rotary Club of Fair Park (Dallas), Texas in1959, served as president in 1965-66 and really couldn't tell you that we did anything more important than giving a $500.00 scholarship each year to some worthy high school student. We met each Thursday for lunch, usually heard a good speaker, then shook hands and said, "See you next week!"

Then in the spring of 1979, an announcement was made at our club that the governor of Rotary District 252 in Sindei, Japan, would like to send 16 boys and girls to the United States for a summer vacation, to spend about 10 days each in Los Angeles, Dallas, and Chicago. They called the program "Wings of Rotary." In return they would host 16 of our students in Japan for up to three weeks. We had a 16-year old son at home who didn't care about going to Japan, but we all thought it would be fun to participate by hosting a student.

From the time we met Jun Hatakyama at the airport, when he bowed and handed us a Japanese-American dictionary, until he tearfully left 10 days later, we got a pleasant taste of what Rotary was about. This led to the development of a Rotary Youth Exchange program in our district the next year.

One of the few things that I remember from my Psychology I01 course at the University of Texas, was that "the first law of mankind is self-preservation"...in other words, if you don't look out for yourself, no one else will. Seemed like good advice. It followed that one should get the best job available out of college, make enough money to be able to get married and support a family, accumulaate enough to "live like the Rileys", make some good investments, and then concentrate on making more money! Man, that took up almost all of one's waking hours and left little time for looking out for anyone else.

Somewhere along the line, the axiom "It's better to give than to receive" kept popping into my head. How can that make sense? Then a Jun Hatakyama came into our lives, and we realized that it is impossible to give and not receive...and sometimes in much greater proportion!

One of the objectives of this book is that it will "turn on the light switch" for Rotarians, spouses, and non-Rotarians alike, as they read the stories of those dedicated Rotarians who have received much more than they have given by having been involved in serving others. Hopefully, as you read these vignettes, you'll think, "Gee, I could do that" or "Wouldn't that be fun?"

I hope that you enjoy it!

TABLE OF CONTENTS

1

GENESIS

....in the beginning

The year was 1872. A lone gas light was burning when a passenger train approached Wallingford, Vt. A three year old boy was scared to death because a father, in financial difficulties, was bringing his son to live with Grandpa and Grandma. When the train stopped, a solitary figure waited for the boy to get off. As Grandpa helped the boy off, he put down his thumb to take his small hand like a security blanket. They walked up the street to his grandparent's house. This was the beginning of a mentoring process that would nurture the first Service Club in the world.

Wallingford was a small town. Paul Harris grew up never knowing a stranger. Grandpa knew everybody. Whenever there was trouble like sickness, injury, lack of food, shelter, Grandma was the servant to the community. Grandpa was of Puritan descent. He lived the Golden Rule. He was honest, frugal, fair, and a hard working man of God. He was an environmentalist. He loved to fish and hunt but only for their needs. The rest was turned back not to be wasted. Education was very important. From the time of reason, Paul was encouraged to think and plan for a college education.

His mind unconsciously was being planted with the philosophy of his environment. The values of the grandparents. The nurture of the community. The beauty of the green hills of Vermont.

Paul did go on to college. He returned to Wallingford before his freshman year was completed due to his grandfather's death. Paul was devastated. He vowed to remain at home to take care of Grandma. Grandma's wisdom prevailed. She reasoned with him that to honor Grandpa, Paul needed to finish his college education. Instead of returning to the Eastern school, he enrolled at the University of Iowa to study law. When Paul completed his law studies, a professor suggested that before he put out his shingle, he travel for five years to get a feel for different kinds of people.

Paul's adventures led him to Montana to work on a ranch, to San Francisco to be a newspaper reporter, and to southern California to work in the fruit harvest. Denver recruited him as an actor. Back across the mountains to work again as a cattle hand. He spent some time in Mississippi boxing fruit. A friend in the granite business called him to work in Jacksonville, Florida. He knew stone from his days in New England. He was successful, so his company sent him to Baltimore, Maryland to open a branch office. Living by the sea, his wanderlust said, "Lets go to Europe."

A cattle company that transported cows to England hired him as a deck hand. The trip was rough but the sights of England beckoned him back. He returned on another boat and this time traveled France, Germany and Italy before returning home. Upon returning to Mississippi to box more fruit, he realized that his five years were up. Chicago was the booming town of America at the turn of the century, so Paul headed for the Windy City to put out his shingle. During the late 1890's, less tthan 5% of people ever traveled more than 30 miles from home. Paul was a world traveler by most standards.

Chicago was a booming business town, but there were no business ethics. Business people lied and cheated. They were afraid to have close friends for fear that they would divulge company secrets. The motto of the day was "Let the buyer beware!" This environment was totally foreign to young Paul. He longed for the days of Wallingford, Vt. He dreamed of having close friends. He couldn't do business without honesty and integrity. He longed for community, where he could help those in need. He was very discouraged.

One day a client invited him to his home in a Chicago suburb for a Sunday dinner. After dinner as they walked the streets in the neighborhood, his friend was continually waving greetings to his friends, awakening Paul's senses to his former roots in Wallingford. An idea started to form, but it took some time to mature.

On February 23, 1905, he gathered three business friends -- Silvester Schiele, Gustavus Loehr and Hiram Shorey -- to share his idea of the first Service Club. The object of this small group was to form friendships, help each other in business and to provide a service to the community.

They called the club Rotary, because they rotated their meetings among each other's offices. The first Service Club in the world had been born. It's motto, "He Profits Most Who Serves Best" is still a beacon for personal, business, community and world relationships.

Today, in its ninety-fourth year, Rotary has approximately 1,200,000 members in 30,000 Rotary Clubs located in 160 countries throughout the world. We have come a long way from the seed planting of the Puritan spirit instilled into young Paul by Grandma and Grandpa Harris.

PDG James L. (Jim) Griffith

Jim Griffith is a member of the Rotary Club of Dallas, Texas. He joined Rotary in Davenport, Iowa in 1961, and the Dallas Club when he moved in 1964. Jim served as president in 1978-79. Most recently, he served Rotary International as Regional Foundation Coordinator from 1997-1999, and is presently a Foundation Permanent Fund National Advisor. Jim was the recipient of the prestigious Rotary International Service Above Self Award in 1997.

2

WORLD COMMUNITY SERVICE

"World Community Service (WCS) is the Rotary program by which a club or district in one country provides humanitarian assistance to a club in another country. Typically, the aid goes to a developing community where the Rotary project will help raise the standard of living and the quality of life. The ultimate object of World Community Service is to build goodwill and understanding among peoples of the world."

....from the ABCs of Rotary

PDG Jim Fitzgerald

James M. (Jim) Fitzgerald has been a member of the Marshall, Texas Rotary Club since 1980, serving as president in 1985. His classification is Mechanical Engineering, and he is the owner of Magnum Machine & Manufacturing Company in Marshall. Jim served as District Governor of Rotary District 5830 in 1991-92.

"It was the most incredible experience of my life. Our flight took us along the coast of Alaska, the Bering Sea, and the coast of Russia. I did not get much sleep on that part of the trip. The sleeplessness came from the unbelievable beauty of the frozen, snow-covered landscape below and the golden "twilight" that lasted for almost eight hours.

As I looked down from 39,000 feet, at that beautiful, yet desolate and foreboding landscape, I wondered how anyone could survive in such extreme cold. I thought of how helpless I would be, and how little hope I would have for survival if the plane were forced to land, or even worse to crash in this desolate, freezing arctic wasteland.

My wife, Georganna, and I were traveling to the Philippines with Dr. Alberto Dela Cruz, a surgeon from the Rotary Club of Winnsboro, Texas. We were going there to dedicate 10 artesian water wells and 10 public restrooms in the city of Orani Bataan, and to participate in a surgical mission organized by Dr. Dela Cruz.

The wells and restrooms were funded through a Rotary Foundation Matching Grant during my year as District Governor. The project was a joint project of three Rotary clubs....Orani, Mandaleyong East, and Winnsboro. They were dug and constructed in 10 separate areas of the city called Barangays, with voluntary labor provided by the Rotarians of Orani Bataan. Nothing I can say would ever adequately express the gratitude and joy that was evident in the faces of the people of Orani, young and old, for those facilities.

At an official ceremony dedicating the wells and restrooms, we accepted a commendation from the city of Orani, on behalf of the Rotarians in the three clubs and all Rotarians of District 5830 and 3800. In addition, Georganna and I were officially adopted by the city of Orani. We now have 45,000 new cousins in the Philippines.

After the formal ceremony was over, we went to the medical mission in Orani to assist the medical team at the little clinic. By the time it was over, between two and three hundred people had been treated, including those who had surgeries for goiters, hernias, cataracts, cysts, and cleft pallets; for medical conditions such as skin diseases, respiratory diseases, and malnutrition; for diagnostic evaluations and follow ups on previous surgeries, and many others too numerous to mention. A total of 20 doctors were involved in the mission which lasted four very long (18 hour) days, not counting the follow up visits that were made the following week.

The mission had to be delayed and almost cancelled when deadly typhoon Lela roared through the Philippines as we were preparing to depart for Orani. I wish every Rotarian in the world could have been with me as I sat at my host's breakfast table that morning, while the team of Rotarians and surgeons agonized over the risk of being trapped in the typhoon on the way to the clinic, if they left as planned. I wish you could have seen the disappointment on the faces and in the hearts of those doctors and Rotarians when the decision was made to delay the mission one day in order to let the typhoon pass. They had committed that week from their medical practices and businesses for this mission. But their concern was not about their practice or business, but that they might not be able to treat all the people who needed their help. I was deeply moved by their commitment to the project, and I was equally impressed by the way the work was accomplished when they arrived the following day.

The sacrifice of the physicians and support people who planned and implemented the mission was staggering. One of the anesthesiologists from Springfield, Ohio, brought cardiac monitoring equipment with him from the United States. Dr. Dela Cruz brought $6,000 worth of surgical equipment and supplies (instruments, gloves, sutures, gowns, and miscellaneous supplies for the operations.) An additional $20,000 worth of medicines and drugs were dispensed free of charge during the mission.

Tuesday evening, December 7, while I spoke to the Rotary Club of Orani, the medical mission continued into the night and following morning (3:00 am.) The medical team was back at work at 8:00 am for another grueling 18-hour day. This went on for the rest of the week. By the end of the mission, not one person who had been scheduled for treatment had gone untreated.

While the mission continued at Orani, Georganna and I proceeded to Subic Bay on Wednesday, December 8. We were given a VIP tour of the abandoned naval station, which was being restored and refurbished for commercial use.

We visited a school for the Deaf and Mute near Subic Bay, which was started and supported by personnel from the naval station up until the base was closed. The school has since been adopted by several Rotary clubs in the area, who send them donations every month to help pay the salaries of the four or five staff members. Along with several volunteers, they operate the school on a budget of approximately $500 per month.

We toured the class rooms where we observed, and sometimes cried, as the children struggled to produce sounds they could not hear, and we cheered and clapped for them when they succeeded. The children even gave us an impromptu demonstration of singing and dancing, using sign language and "mouthing" the words. The first song was the "Lord's Prayer," and there was not a dry eye in the crowd when they finished.

Just down the street from the school, we visited a Rotary Village Corps project sponsored by the Rotarians of Olongapo. This was a "Skills Development Training Center" for teaching sewing skills to people in that depressed area, so they could get jobs in garment factories nearby.

It seemed like a lifetime, but we had been there only FIVE days!

The balance of the trip was filled with Rotary functions, including seeing a Rotary Mobile X-ray unit in action on its monthly visit to a distressed neighborhood, handing out Christmas gifts to children at an orphanage, some golf and a little shopping, but mostly driving in traffic, so impossible as to try the patience of "Job".

On the flight back to Marshall, Texas, USA, my thoughts turned to the people of Orani, Bataan, Philippines, and of how little hope they had for life at all, much less a healthy life. I thought of how Rotary had been there, even before I had heard of their needs, and even before the clubs in our district had gotten involved in the effort to help them. There were Rotarians helping those unfortunate people survive in a world every bit as hostile to them as the Arctic Tundra would have been to me.

To be sure, I could never have survived in the Arctic winter wasteland without help, and neither could those people in the Philippines have survived without help from Rotary!

I first met Cameron Gray in June, 1985. I was "making-up" Rotary at the Garland Lakeside (TX) meeting, and the program for the day was to be given by a Rotarian from Grand Prairie, TX, one of our district clubs. It was presented by Judge Cameron Gray, whom everyone calls Cam.

Cam was a Justice of Peace and held court on three different week-days in three separate communities under his jurisdiction. The unique feature of his court was that juveniles in each of these communities who committed minor offenses (misdemeanors) were referred to his court and, according to the severity of the offense, the juvenile was sentenced to a certain number of hours or days with the Sanitation Department of that community, cleaning up the streets and highways. The court gained wide-spread attention, and the idea was picked up by other communities.

Three years later, our paths crossed again. I found out that, in addition to his duties as J.P., Cam had been making several trips to Central America, primarily to El Salvador. Here is where his story picks up:

Cameron Gray

During 1985, while attending my Grand Prairie Rotary Club, I heard a speaker who told about the ravages of a civil war raging in El Salvador. After his presentation, I talked at some length with the speaker, who told me that there was a great need for people to adopt children who had lost their parents in the war. It was during that period of time that Mary and I were looking at the possibility of adoption. I decided to take a trip with some other members of a church group to learn more about the war and of the possibilities of adoption.

When I toured El Salvador for the first time, I was overwhelmed by the tragedy of the war. Children as young as six years of age were living alone in cardboard boxes. Starvation and malnutrition existed everywhere in the conflictive zones. There was inadequate or nonexistent medical treatment for children. I came back to the United States profoundly impacted by what I had heard and seen. I was shocked into the reality of extreme suffering and wanted to do something to help make a difference.

I started collecting and shipping supplies to El Salvador, with the assistance of churches and other Rotary clubs. I used the money I collected from weddings to pay for my expenses. I slowly developed some very strong and lasting friendships with other Rotarians living in El Salvador. They were helpful with my problems in customs and assisted me in the delivery of supplies. Working in the war with my fellow Rotarians was a wonderful and fulfilling experience. This was the true spirit of Rotary -- people helping people. After years of experience, the word began to spread in charity circles about the work of Rotary in El Salvador. We were asked to help other charities with the projects. By the end of the civil war, we had developed a strong reputation for providing assistance to the poor.

It was during this period that I also developed some important relationships with Rotarians living in the United States. One of the most important persons was a Rotarian by the name of Marshall Mackler, who serves on the board of directors of Christian Relief Services in Lorton, Virginia. Marshall used his contacts to help us send 40-foot shipping containers filled with relief supplies to El Salvador. The staff at CRS was extremely helpful in assisting our work in El Salvador, and that helpfulness has extended to this day with our work in Eastern Europe, Mexico, and all of Central America. We could have never accomplished what has been done without the invaluable help of Marshall and the staff at CRS. Special mention goes to staff members Jenny Patterson and her able assistant, Laura Johnson. Yet another example of how networking with Rotarians has made a big difference in the lives of so many people.

Another Rotarian who would be hard to forget is the former chairman of the board of Gift of Life, Inc., Kurt Weishaupt. Gift of Life, Inc., is a non-profit entity organized by Rotary District 7250 in New York. Kurt called me one day out of the blue and offered a donation of $1,000,000 in medical aid for the people of El Salvador. He had previously been a large contributor to Russia and wanted to expand to other countries. His initial offer grew to $5,000,000! Kurt is one of the most sensitive and generous men I have ever known. The last time I spoke with Kurt, he was in his mid-eighties and still going strong. His secretary told me that he still drives his car to work every day and that his office is a mess, with papers strewn all over the floor. However he did it, it was the results that counted!

The years between 1990 and the present have been filled with more and more contacts, resulting in the expansion of a relief oganization which I had developed, called "Orphans of the World, Inc." In November, 1998, our work moved into a rapid pace due to the events of Hurricane Mitch in Central America. Our years of experience with Rotarians in Central America made it easy for us to accommodate the shipments of emergency supplies to the Mitch victims.

On the heels of Mitch came the crisis in Kosovo. So far, we have been able to send seven ocean containers to the refugees living in Tirana, Albania.

On October 26, 1998, the day after the beginning of the devastation wrought by Hurricane Mitch, Rotary District 5810 was setting its disaster relief program in motion. Pete Snider, District Director of International Service, picks up the story from here:

Pete Snider, Asst. Gov. District 5810

Pete Snider joined the Rotary Club of Balch Springs (TX) in 1991. He served as President 1996-97, as District Director of International Service 1997-98, and is presently an Assistant Governor of District 5810.

"I've got this friend." How many times have I heard it? That phrase always seems to be the lead-in to a greater understanding of what can happen when people go beyond themselves. This time it touched me deeply because it represented so many people and such great need. The need was that which was created by "Hurricane Mitch", when it caused so much devastation in Latin America. It has been described as the worst disaster and loss of human lives in the Western Hemisphere during the 20th century. It started with 150 mile-per-hour winds that wracked most of Honduras. The greatest damage and loss of lives, however, was due to the effect of six days of torrential rains, which literally caused mountains to crumble, covering up entire communities. That was the emergency!

"I've got this friend" begins with Milton Kessel, PDG of District 5810.

Milton was looking for means to mount a meaningful effort to help the people of Honduras. Seventy per cent of its arable land had been washed away, countless homes and much of the country's infrastructure had been destroyed.

The "friend" here was Cameron Gray, who headed a relief agency in Grand Prairie, Texas called "Orphans of the World." Cam, a former lawyer and judge, had been active in Central America for many years. I became aware that Cam was a genuine humanitarian in every sense of the word. He now spends a lot of time on a forklift, loading relief supplies. Or he may be trekking through the jungles of Central America to bring some hope and opportunity to people who desperately need it.

When Cam was asked how we could go about getting supplies to Honduras, he said, "I've got this friend", who turned out to be Rotarian Marshall Mackler, on the board of Christian Relief Services of Lorton, Virginia. Cam had previously used those contacts to arrange for free shipment of goods to places they were needed so badly. Contact with Marshall led us to the shippers, Sealand and Dole, who were to provide us with the same needed service.

Our then District Governor, Bill Frew, contacted RI and District Governor Mario Valdes, whose district covers Honduras. Governor Valdes "had these friends", Tony Medina and Carlos Flores. Carlos was the chief officer in charge of the Port of San Pedro Sula, the only operating port in Honduras. He was to expedite all of our shipments.

As a result of concerted effort by a number of Rotarians in our district, we raised $48,000 within ten days. We realized that the most urgent need was for food. Again, Milton said, "I've got this friend." He was PDG J. B. Roberts from Plainview, Texas, in a near-by district. J. B. directed us to a dehydrated food manufacturer in Lubbock, Texas. Another "friend" Rotarian delivered over 30 pallets of the food (864# each) to us on three separate shipments at no cost. We found a source of powdered milk in East Texas, and District Governor Bob Young of District 5830 arranged to have the shipment picked up and delivered to us at no cost.

Other "friends" were discovered. One was Dr. Jim DuBus, whose father had been a rice broker. We were directed to Riceland Foods in Stuttgart, Arkansas. The CEO of Riceland, Bill Reed, is the current president of the Stuttgart Rotary Club. Bill and his "friend" John Lorich from DeWitt, Arkansas, and along with their two clubs, joined in to ship the rice to us. We were able to purchase and transport this much needed staple for two cents a serving!

Once we were able to get this snowball rolling, we found ourselves in the midst of a full-blown avalanche! Cam had been contacted by Luis Guiterrez of the Honduras Association of Dallas to help ship donated goods to Honduras. They had collected several trailer loads of clothes, medical supplies, canned food and bottled water. However, they had no way to move the goods except by trucking it overland all the way to Honduras at $6,000 per truckload. Cam Gray's comment was, "They really collected some good stuff and we'll find a way to deliver it." Orphans of the World was able to deliver it all, and it was distributed by Rotarians in Honduras at absolutely no cost. After the first 15 containers went out, Cam started shipping to Nicaragua and El Salvador.

Since that awful storm, we have bought and shipped $22,000 worth of emergency food as part of the 30, fully-loaded, 40-foot ocean containers we shipped in a matter of sixty days. We have gathered and sorted over 650 tons of food, medicine and clothing with an estimated value of well over a million dollars! Two Rotarians in our district traveled great distances to see that things actually got where they were needed. Tino Trulillo, PP of the Plano Rotary Club, left shortly after the hurricane to assess the damage. Frank Casero, President-elect of the Carrollton-Farmers Branch club, went to Panama for a meeting with Rotarians from throughout Central America to discuss plans for rebuilding. He is now in Central America as a Rotary Volunteer, seeking the best ways to use our remaining funds for long-term rebuilding in Honduras, El Salvador and Nicaragua.

In the middle of this almost unbelievable effort, District Governor Bill Frew was working to direct our efforts for matching grants from Rotary International. We are planning to build twenty-four basic homes In Honduras and do it with the tools supplied by Rotary. We are providing propane stoves in Nicaragua in an area that is rapidly becoming deforested by people cutting wood for cooking. We will help to equip a trade school in El Salvador which is training diesel mechanics.

After a very busy year working with caring Rotarians from our district and around the world, I re-read the Object of Rotary. What it means to me is, "I've got these friends!"

The MediSend Program

Although the program has been a humanitarian effort of District 5810 since July, 1997, there are still a number of Rotarians and others who are not familiar with MediSend, what it is, what it does, and the significant role which it plays in World Community Service.

Waldo Cecil, a member of the Irving, TX Rotary Club, introduced the MediSend Program to the district, when he asked for and received the approval of the then District Governor Herb Kamm, to visit Rotary Clubs in the district and enlist their financial support for MediSend.

Waldo Cecil

"Since 1990, MediSend International has shipped more than 200 tons of medical supplies and equipment valued at more than $6.5 million dollars to some 57 nations around the world. The backlog of requests continues to grow as the knowledge of MediSend's work spreads throughout the developing nations of the world. While MediSend International was able to collect surplus medical supplies and equipment, the one element needed to complete the cycle was not available....the money to pay for the shipments to the foreign countries.

The goal of District 5810 was to make MediSend an on-going, permanent district project, with an annual contribution by the various participating clubs of $30,000. The first year (1997-98), contributions totalled $20,000 plus. At the end of the 1998-99 year, the yearly total was slightly over $27,000. The financial goal of $30,000 converts into $60,000 through the Matching Grant program of Rotary International. That amount provides the funds for an average of eight shipments per year valued at over $1,000,000.

The beneficiaries of these supplies are hospitals throughout the world, where urgent needs exist. By the end of the second year, one shipment was made to the Victoria Hospital in Jinetoga, Nicaragua. At this writing, five matching grants are in the works, with three of them already approved. The other two will follow shortly, with shipments going to Kenya, Honduras, Indonesia, Belarus, and Sri Lanka. There is sufficient money in The MediSend Program account to begin seeking additional matching grants in the early months of the fiscal year 99/00.

Ruth Dynbort, Executive Director of MediSend International says, "Rotary International has a long and well-deserved global reputation in health care. District 5810 may well be initiating the next Rotary International global project for the 21st Century. MediSend International is honored to have such a distinguished partner."

MediSend/International

In the "globalized" world of the next century, the resources of private institutions will be shared to help people reduce economic and physical waste and eventually change the way that governments operate. MediSend/International has been working since 1990 to collect surplus medical supplies and equipment in the United States for distribution to public and charity hospitals in developing countries. The American health care system discards over $6.25 billion of medical surplus each year; materials that are past sterile date, materials opened but never used, working equipment replaced by newer technology. These materials sit in warehouses or find their way to landfills. Meanwhile, in poorer nations, standard medical materials like surgical gloves and sutures are too precious to throw away. The surplus that is an environmental and economic burden in the United States can provide immeasurable hope and healing overseas.

The long-term vision of MediSend/International is to change the nature of public health in the developing world by providing materials for the infrastructure of health care. The money that governments save through our donations of surplus can be used to provide preventive health services to all citizens of a nation, especially the indigent. This vision compels our Board of Directors to make an enormous time commitment to MediSend/International; their leadership has a direct impact upon the growth of our organization. The MediSend/International staff, who are experienced non-profit professionals, choose to work for us because they can see the immediate results of our work in communities around the world. MediSend/International's optimistic mission has attracted thousands of volunteers and supporters over the years -- medical professionals who collect materials and serve as volunteer ambassadors, community members from all walks of life who sort, inventory and pack items at our donated warehouse; and corporations, individuals and partner organizations who assist our programs with financial gifts. The members of the "MediSend Family" participate in healing the world, one shipment at a time.

MediSend/International was founded by Dr. Martin Lazar, a Dallas neurosurgeon who was both morally and professionally compelled to respond to the discrepancy between the resources of health care facilities in the developing world and those in the U.S.

MediSend/International is a non-political, non-sectarian, non-profit organization. We donate to qualified medical institutions based on their financial status and population served, and regardless of any religious, ethnic or other affiliation. The efficiency with which MediSend/International operates ensures that over 93% of our budget is devoted to our actual program of turning leftovers into lifesavers.

Contributions by individuals and corporations, and grants from private foundations and the federal government, comprise the funding that MediSend/International receives. In FY99, MediSend/International received over $100,000 in grants. Gifts in kind in FY99 were in excess of $200,000. Financial support is vital for the continuation of both our domestic collections program and the international distribution program, as well as for the establishment of a development office.

We invite you to join our "Lifeline of Hope" in the globalized century ahead.

Send-A-Book

In 1995, Sid Barnard, a member of the Rotary Club of Richardson, Texas, was the catalyst in the development of Rotary District 5810's Send-A-Book project. He visited almost every club in the district to tell of the urgent need for the program. Here is his story:

Sid Barnard

In 1983, my wife, Ruth and I, flew to the Philippines to begin our new lives serving as missionaries to the people there. We would be primarily in the rural areas of the central islands. Our work offered us the opportunity to visit many schools, city schools as well as small primary schools in mountain barangays. The condition of the schools and their supplies was deplorable. Many schools didn't even have floors; so when it rained (which was often), the ground was just covered with mud. Even in the more affluent cities, school libraries had very low priorities.

I saw a desperate need for books and began to look for ways to meet those needs. Everywhere I looked, I was met with utter frustration. I found sources of books in the United States and found that the United States Navy would transport the books for free; however, they had to be donated to the Ministry of Education. They proudly insisted they could provide textbooks for their students and did not want our "hand-me-downs." They said they would be more than happy to accept our money, so that they could publish their own books. We tried to find funding and means through churches and missions, but their programs were based primarily in sending religious books and materials.

Birth of Send-A-Book

In 1995, I was invited to join the Richardson, Texas, Rotary Club, with a classification of International Trade. Two weeks after joining the club, I was given a budget of $500 and asked to develop an international project. Send-A-Book was born. University of Texas Dallas offered a lot of books being removed from their shelves. I loaded five large boxes (1,000 books) in my car, drove them to Houston and put them on a ship bound for Cebu, Philippines. Total cost: $500. Enthusiasm in our club for the project was very high. We wanted to do it again and do more.

To expand the project further, I suggested to our District Governor that the program be extended to involve other clubs in the district, and he was enthusiastic about doing this.

We found that there was a plentiful supply of books which had been removed from the shelves in the school systems because of the date of publication; in some cases, they were ready to be scrapped. The books were offered to us at no-charge. Our responsibility was to pick them up, package them in boxes, make arrangements for shipping, and deliver to the shipper. The out-of-pocket cost was the shipping cost, itself.

During 1997, we shipped five, 40-ft. containers (almost 200,000 books) with a total published value of over $1,500,000! This has become a yearly project for many of the clubs in the district.

I have traveled to the Philippines each year since 1995. The distribution of the books is in the hands of the Philippine Rotary Clubs, and I wanted to be a part of it. The Rotarians were more than willing to let me share their job in passing out the books. It was a thrill to watch a library full of school kids poring over their bonanza of new schoolbooks.

Negros and Siquejor Islands are made up mostly of rural towns and villages. Yet the 10 Rotary Clubs there distributed more than 50,000 books last year. I wasn't there to see them in action, but they told me of traveling to mountain villages, carrying the books on the back of their motorcycles, taking boxes of books from island to island by ferry boat, bouncing their rough, rocky roads and fording creeks to reach some book-hungry kids and teachers. Their questions, "When can we get more books?"

So, what should we tell them? Do we let this excitement wane? Do we drop the project? Or do we keep trying until we find the right way to do it and keep on going? I wish that more of our Rotarians could see that excitement! It would be wonderful if some of them took the opportunity to go over there and see what our pennies are buying for these kids.

Dr. John Petty, Rotary District 5830

Dr. Petty is a member of the Rotary Club of Longview, Texas. He joined the club in March, 1995, under the classification of Chiropractor. Shortly thereafter, he was selected to be the Team Leader of a Group Study Exchange Team to Venezuela. He is currently president-elect.

Rotarians in the United States and other prosperous countries can help save and improve lives in less fortunate part of the world by tapping a little-known and under-utilized resource. Valuable items of perfectly serviceable medical equipment are retired every day by hospitals, clinics and physicians: dialysis units, fetal monitors, hospital beds, examination tables, x-ray units, stethoscopes, ophthalmoscopes--an endless list. It happens when newer models or methods come along and when health-care businesses close, typically due to declining viability in some areas or retirement of physicians. There is virtually no market for much of this equipment, and depreciation has reduced its book value to zero for charitable tax deduction purposes. Many of them are eager to donate such equipment for reputable worthy causes if properly approached.

A Venezuelan Adventure

This story begins in Longview, Texas, in April 1996, when I was asked to lead a Rotary Group Study Exchange team from District 5830 to Venezuela. While being hosted by the Rotary Club of Guarapiche in the city of Maturin, the team saw great needs in the medical community. The city of 400,000 had a total of four dialysis machines. People were dying of kidney failure while they awaited their turns for treatment. Another great need was obvious in the city of Puerto Ordaz, where the local Rotary club was assisting in planning and constructing a small new clinic. The small facility, supervised by the Red Cross and operated by Rotary, was to serve ten percent of the 400,000 people in the combined cities of Puerto Ordaz and San Felix. Puerto Ordaz Rotarian Henry Beermude gave the visiting team a five-page want list of medical needs.

After returning home, I mounted a campaign to locate the equipment.

It was a difficult process to even find the right person to ask, but finally the responses began to come in from nearby east Texas towns. One reason for the success of this project was the high regard for the good name of Rotary. No one was being asked to give equipment and supplies to a private organization which often extracts high service charges. Rotary delivered the equipment where it was needed and did so with a minimum of cost.

I contacted Dr. James Cotton of the Watson Wise Dialysis Center in Tyler, a unit of the Renal Care Group based in Nashville, Tennessee. Dr. Cotton was pleased to place the much needed dialysis units in the respected hands of Rotary. There were units left over to be shared with other needy areas. The total value of this equipment was a million dollars.

During 1997, we had to deal with another problem -- how were we going to transport this equipment to Venezuela? The Rotarians found out about a U.S. government policy called the Denton Amendment program, which allowed humanitarian aid materials to be carried without charge on American military aircraft on a space-available basis.

The dialysis units arrived in December, 1997 and the Rotary District Governor there arranged for them to be picked up at the Venezuelan military air base at Maracay, near Caracas, to be distributed in Maharin and locations in 11 other cities in District 4370.

Providing equipment and supplies for the Puerto Ordaz hospital was a separate project. The biggest single out-of-pocket expense was $700 for commercial delivery of the equipment in a 53-foot trailer from Longview to Mobile, Alabama. It was then packed into three, 20-foot seagoing containers and shipped on a Venezuelan cargo ship returning from Mobile. It also arrived in December, 1997 and was stored by Rotarians, pending the completion of the hospital during the following summer.

Delivery of all of the equipment was supervised by local Rotarians, assuring that it was to be used for humanitarian purposes in the intended locations, without profit and without charge beyond nominal expenses.

The entire operation took hundreds of hours of hard work by Rotarians in this country and in Venezuela. I was asked to go to Venezuela in January, 1998, to attend the ceremonies dedicating the dialysis units at locations in four cities. Among others present were Assistant U.S. Ambassador John Keane, Venezuelan Secretary of State Jose Andueze, Governor Didalco Boliva of the State of Aragua.

It is wonderful to have the personal feeling of doing good for a lot of people; however, it was only because of Rotary that the project was successfully completed.

All Rotarians recognize community service as one of the four "Avenues of Service" in Rotary. Since Rotary exists in over 160 countries in the world, "community" has been extended to include not only the local community but the communities of the world.

Rotarians representing all businesses and professions have found much personal satisfaction in extending their services to needy inhabitants in countries other than their own. Many Rotarians, particularly in the medical field, spend anywhere from one to four weeks of what might have otherwise been their vacation, to perform highly important services in foreign countries.

One of these Rotarians who has made such noteworthy trips for a number of years is Dr. Tom Brian, D.D.S. , a member of the Rotary Club of Allen, Texas. Here's what Tom has to say about his contribution to World Community Service:

Tom Brian, D.D.S.

It is always exciting for me each year to see what the new Rotary motto will be. In a few short words, the RI President says a lot about himself and his hopes for all Rotarians.

One of my favorites was President Cliff Dochterman's theme, "Real

Happiness is Helping Others." For you see, in 1991, I discovered the deep satisfaction of serving others through my vocation, dentistry. It was that year that I was introduced to a man who joined our church, and then invited me to go to Honduras to work with a medical/dental team. We worked on the eastern side of Honduras, the Moskito Coast, and treated the Moskito Indians.

La Mosquitia is the very poorest part of one of the poorest countries in Central America. There are no roads connecting the east side with the higher populated western side. No roads means no electrical or telephone lines and difficulty in transporting goods. People travel on pothole-infested dirt roads or by boat. Medical care is minimal and dental care is non-existent. After seeing the need, I returned to La Mosquitia the next year and now make at least three trips there annually.

In addition to Honduras, I have also worked in Mexico, Guatemala, and Peru. I usually make about eight trips a year, ranging from a long week-end to ten days.

On a trip in 1995, I saw a boy walking with the aid of a stick he was holding in front of him. At first glance I thought that he was simply playing with the stick, but after taking a closer look, I realized that he was crippled in one leg and using the stick to walk. When I asked a nurse about him, I was informed that he had an accident eight years ago and had never received treatment. It took me a year to find someone to treat him, to find out how to get the boy a visa and get him to Texas. Since then, seven other children have received orthopedic surgery in Dallas, some at the world-famous Texas Scottish Rite Children's Hospital.

A continuous need in La Mosquitia is for school supplies. At the end of each school year, an effort is made to collect all of the crayons, notebooks, scissors, pencils, glue, etc. that our local students discard. These items are sorted, packed and shipped to the Moskito area, along with smaller amounts of medicine and food. My church has collected shoes, bicycles, teddy bears, and Christmas gifts as well. I had been working with a U.S. military program to ship 28,000 pounds of supplies to La Mosquitia just before Hurricane Mitch hit Honduras. I was able to get those supplies shipped quickly to help in the relief effort after the hurricane.

Presently, I am working on a Matching Grant from RI to fund the drilling of a water well. Much of my volunteer efforts are not done under the auspices of Rotary International. However, "Real happiness *is* helping others" and this is what Rotary is all about.

A RUSSIAN ODESSEY

Jim Aneff, Abilene Southwest (TX) Rotary Club

Jim has been a member of Rotary since 1979, and served as president of his club in 1984-85. Before becoming involved with Rotary's International Youth Exchange program, he was with another international youth program. He was one of the founding members of SCRYE (South Central Rotary Youth Exchange). Jim has been involved in many other facets of Rotary, and tells us about an exciting Rotary adventure.

"The most fascinating thing to me about Rotary International is that it provides individuals the opportunity to serve in ways one could never imagine.

With the end of the Cold War and the reaching out of Rotary to once forbidden places, I became involved in one of the most interesting adventures of service in my life. Along the way, I have made new friends from such places as Fairbanks and Anchorage to Magadan, Vladivostok and Chita.

It all began in 1995. For ten years I had been involved in a Rotary multi-district youth exchange organization called South Central Rotary Youth Exchange, Inc. (SCRYE). Earlier in 1995, PDG Alan Hoener, a past president of SCRYE, helped found a Rotary youth exchange organization called U.S.-Canada Rotary Youth Exchange Conference. As a result of new contacts, SCRYE was invited to host two Rotary exchange students from Vladivostok, Russia. At the same time we learned that R.I. President Herbert G. Brown scheduled a regional Rotary Conference in Anchorage, Alaska, called a Russian Peace Forum, to be held that October. The purpose was to discuss the development of Rotary in the Russian Far East and Siberia. Yes, Siberia....of all places! I decided to attend since SCRYE was hosting students from that area.

At the conference I met 60 new Rotarians from places all over Siberia and the Russian Far East. I learned that there were direct flights from Alaska to several cities in this vast unknown land. But how could a simple Rotarian from Abilene, Texas, make any contribution in Siberia? I left the conference with the feeling that perhaps our Rotary club could "throw a little money" at a Rotary Foundation matching grant project or host an exchange student. That was all I could visualize.

Then, during Christmas, 1995, D. G. Jack Randolph from Alaska called. His Rotary District 5010 is responsible for development of Rotary in this part of Russia, which encompasses eleven time zones. He invited our Rotary club to sponsor the Rotary Club of Chita, a city of 400,000 people, located north of Mongolia in Southern Siberia. In the same breath he asked if I could accompany him on a chartering trip through Siberia and the Russian Far East in April, 1996. I thought he was joking. To my amazement, he was serious. It took 10 minutes for our Rotary club Board of Directors to approve the project. It took me two months to prepare for the journey.

From Anchorage, we flew over the Bering Sea and four hours later landed in the cold northern city of Magadan. This city was used by Stalin as the administrative headquarters for the infamous Russian Siberian Gulag. A Rotary Club had been chartered there the previous year, and our group of Rotarians, along with the Magadan Rotary Club, were going to a small remote town named Palatka about two hours away to charter another club. We arrived at the town meeting hall for the ceremonies and dinner. Besides meeting wonderful people, the thing which struck me with awe was to see, displayed on six, blue felt-covered 4'x4' boards, small Rotary Club banners from clubs of many countries, including one from my Abilene Southwest Rotary Club! That previous fall in Anchorage, we had exchanged banners at the Russian Peace Forum. For the first time, I truly understood the meaning of Rotary Club banners. I looked at them displayed in such a remote town in Siberia, isolated for the last 75 years from the outside world. There I realized that through the miracle of Rotary, individuals from Palatka had made personal contact with Rotarians, clubs, cities and countries stretching from Australia and Japan to the United States and Canada.

As I stood there, I felt a sense of belonging to a much larger world. For these people, they would no longer be isolated from the rest of the world, with the arrival of Rotary and the available use of the internet to communicate freely with new-found friends.

But the real beginning of my Russian experience was the development of close personal relationships with the Chita Rotary Club. Our sponsorship of this club has lead one step at a time to a far greater service than any of us could have planned. Here are some of the things which have resulted from this ever-expanding experience: (1) Our club members have formed close personal friendships with many of the Chita Rotarians, and we continue to communicate frequently. A delegation of eleven Rotarians from Chita came to Abilene and was hosted by our club, as well as by the other two Rotary Clubs in Abilene. (2) After the Chita delegation came to Abilene, our mayor asked us to help sponsor a group of Russian businessmen under a special program called the Productivity Enhancement Program sponsored by the Center for Citizens Initiative in San Francisco. Eleven Russian businessmen came for one month, and more than 500 people in Abilene were involved in that project. We hosted the first Rotary high school exchange student from Chita for one year, and have just completed hosting a second exchange student, as well. (3) We have brought two Russian English teachers to our district to learn how we teach English as a foreign language in our schools. The last Russian teacher conducted classes on Russian culture to over 1,500 students in our schools. (4) Our second teacher from Abilene will go to Chita in the fall of 1999, also through the Rotary Inter-Country Teacher Exchange program. All four of the teachers involved have been funded through Rotary International and our district (5) And most important...eight Rotarians, including several wives from Abilene and two special Rotarians from St. Louis, have now traveled on the Trans-Siberian Railroad, meeting many new friends and helping to sponsor and charter new Rotary Clubs in Siberia.

In 1998 our Rotary District 5790, along with the Dallas District, sponsored ten students from Irkutsk State University for one month to live with families and intern in businesses--to experience how the Free Enterprise System really works. Six are included in the 1999 project and are included in Rotary Club activities. Last year's group returned to their Russian university and persuaded officials to include service projects as a part of the required "service" in their school curriculum. These highly educated students, we believe, will be new

Rotarians when they enter their business careers.

A special contribution was made in the name of a Southwest Rotary Club member, Jack Connor, to help in the development of a memorial and World Peace Center in Magadan, in memory of those thirty-five million Russians who died during Stalin's reign of terror. The center is now open.

But most touching is the dream this whole adventure gave to my dear friend, PDG Alan Hoener from St. Louis, Missouri. At his age of almost 80, his Webster Groves, Missouri Rotary Club celebrated its 75th Rotary anniversary. As a gift to Rotary, Alan wanted his club to charter a club in Siberia. In the spring of 1997, he and Steve LaBarge made a site visit to the town of Aginskoye, located near Mongolia in Southern Siberia, not far from Chita. They completed the long trip on the Trans-Siberian Railroad, participating in the chartering of several new Rotary Clubs and seeing first-hand a land they thought they never would be permitted to visit. Shortly after returning home, Alan went to the Rotary International Convention in Glasgow, Scotland. During that convention, he had a massive heart attack and died.

Alan lived his dream, and his dream has lived on. He was totally intrigued by visiting a part of the world few Westerners have been able to see during this century. He started a project which he knew would be finished. In May, 1998,. Steve LaBarge, representing the Webster Groves Rotary Club, along with a group of us from Abilene and Alaska, chartered the Aginskoye Rotary Club....for Alan.

Alan always signed his letters to me, "Rotarily yours"

For me, Alan's life demonstrated what each of us can do through Rotary which we could not do by ourself. Each Rotarian has special gifts. All we need to do is to be willing to imagine, dream, and act.

One simple "yes" led me on a continuing journey, and along the way others have joined in. Wouldn't it be great if every Rotarian could have as much satisfaction in Rotary and in life as Alan had. We would all be signing our letters, "Rotarily yours."

3

RYLA... ROTARY YOUTH LEADERSHIP AWARDS

Certainly, one of the highlights of my Rotary experiences was the five weeks that Rose and I spent during the spring of 1989 in Rotary District 960, which comprises 55 clubs in the southeastern part of Queensland, Australia. I had been selected as the Team Leader for Rotary's Group Study Exchange to that Rotary District.

As we visited and made our presentations, we heard about a program called, "Rotary Youth Leadership Awards", or RYLA. At each club we visited, we found that the clubs were nominating candidates for their summer RYLA program. They said that it was a summer leadership camp, sponsored by all of the clubs in the district, for young adults, and began in their district in 1965. By 1989, I had been in Rotary for 30 years and had never heard of the program.

When we returned, I explored the RYLA program with several interested Rotarians, and we started our planning for the first camp to be held in June, 1991. Our 9th Annual District 5810 RYLA Camp was held in June, 1999 at Bridgeport, Texas (the original site).

No program of this extent could have become so successful without a group of dedicated Rotarians. There are between 35 and 40 Rotarians each year who make up the RYLA staff of counselors, program planners, and trainers.

The ultimate success of RYLA District 5810 has been due to two highly motivated, outstanding Rotarians who have devoted an inordinate amount of their time and energy for the past nine years to develop this program. They are Dr. Dana Mackison, a member of the Rotary Club of Carrollton, Farmers Branch, Tx, who has been the RYLA district chairman since 1993 and Activities Director for the past nine years, and Mark Healy, Dallas Market Center Club, who has been Camp Director since the second year. These two have provided outstanding organizational and leadership abilities for the program's success.

Dana was a practicing chiropractor for 21 years. During that time, almost all of his "leisure" hours were spent with youth services, Since 1977 he has worked with the Boy Scouts of America, helping with the planning of their National and International Events and Shows. Since 1991, he has devoted much of his time with RYLA.

During the six years as RYLA district chairman, Dana has been in charge of planning the entire schedule of events for the next RYLA Camp. In 1998, Dana was one of only seven Rotarians named to Rotary's International RYLA Committee, set up to develop and extend RYLA to districts throughout the world which have not yet participated At the moment the camp begins, Dana becomes Activities Director, and Mark Healy takes over total charge as Camp Director.

Mark Healy joined the Rotary Club of Pleasant Grove (Dallas) TX in 1989. He is presently a member of the Dallas Market Center Club. He served the district as Vocational Service Chairman from 1995-2000. During the 1999-2000 Rotary year, he is serving District 5810 as an Assistant Governor.

District 5810 has been extremely fortunate to have a Rotarian like Mark to direct this camp for the past eight years. His rapport with the campers has been outstanding. Mark has earned the devotion and admiration of almost 1,000 Rylarians during those years. Here is his exciting story!

Mark Healy

My first knowledge of RYLA came in the fall of 1990, when I was asked by my club president to attend a meeting on a new youth program being developed in our district. No one with my club knew anything about RYLA, and I was interested in finding out what it was. At that meeting, I was asked to serve as a Staff Counselor for the first camp being held the following year. I'm extremely pleased that I said , "Yes."

Clubs were informed about RYLA, and even though to many of the club presidents it was only a "concept", 29 clubs sponsored a total of 48 campers for the first year. The nearest high school to the participating club was contacted by the club, and school counselors were asked to select qualified students. The counselors were told that RYLA was a leadership development program and designed for students who had already demonstrated their leadership qualities in their school activities. They were to be students in their junior year. We asked that at least three students be nominated for each of the slots (several of the clubs wanted to sponsor two students).

The first RYLA Camp was all-male. There were 48 campers sponsored by 29 of the clubs in the District. Seven of the finest young men that I had ever met were in my cabin. The camp was wall-to-wall excitement and a real learning experience for us all. Half of each day was spent in presentations by professionals on important topics, such as Ethics, Leadership and Community Service. The other half of the day was spent outdoors on a myriad of activities, designed to develop the inherent leadership qualities in each of the campers.

I have watched this program grow from 48 young men in our first camp, to 125 male and female campers, 21 Assistant Counselors (Rylarians from previous camps) and 35-40 Rotarian counselor and staff members. And since our first camp, we have gained Rotarians. These are parents who have been so impressed with the change in their son or daughter that they join Rotary, and get involved with RYLA!

I am also proud to say that I have witnessed many powerful young leaders find the keys to succeeding in working with others through RYLA.

In a real sense, I have been the one who has learned from them, and I feel that I am a better person for having known them.

In our effort to make each succeeding camp better than the previous one, we ask the students to evaluate their experiences, with suggestions of how the future camps can be improved. Their replies have been heart-warming and give us support and assurance that we're "on the right track."

Following are excerpts from some of the comments that the Rylarians have made through the years:

"In the summer of 1996, my life was forever changed by the events and people of Camp RYLA. As a painfully shy girl, I entered the warm smiles and handshakes of RYLA with low self-confidence and inability to believe in myself. Little did I know that I was going to exit those same smiles and handshakes a new person with memories and friendships that will last a lifetime. While receiving many "letters from home" at camp, I developed a special bond with the deliverer of those messages, Mark Healy. Though I was unaware at the time, he pushed me to step out of my "comfort zone" each time he called my name to pick up a letter. RYLA helped me to pull through the rough transitions from high school to college. Mark Healy has been an inspiration to everyone that has been in contact with him through RYLA. I can only hope to touch as many lives as he has in such a positive way."

Britnee Reamy, RYLA 1996/Assistant Counselor 1997

"In a world that seems to be turning out the lights on its youth, Camp RYLA shines brightly to lead a new generation on. In my six year involvement with Camp RYLA, I have seen lives change and people grow. Most importantly, I have felt that I have made a difference....a difference that can be passed on to others around the world. Nowhere else can one be filled with knowledge, love and compassion than they can at RYLA. My life has truly been changed. Changed because of a group of people who truly believe in the goodness of the human soul -- Rotarians -- the very people who make RYLA possible. I thank each and every one of them for making me who I am today."

Kevin "Scooter" Ward, RYLA 1994/
A.C. 1995, Staff 1996, 1997, 1998, 1999.

"Hello Mark....I'm John Ahlfors, Tiffany Ahlfor's father, and I want you to know how much Tiffany enjoyed the RYLA Leadership Camp last week. She has not been able to stop talking about it since she returned on Friday. She tells us that (and I quote), "It was the best experience I have ever had in my whole life." Everything that we have heard from her does indicate that it was an extremely positive and uplifting camp and she really seems to be a completely changed person. Our family thanks you for your leadership and time given to the RYLA Camp. It must have been well organized and focused on the messages that were important. Tiffany has said that she would love to attend as an Assistant Counselor next year to help other young people with their positive experiences. Again, thank you for providing and heading-up such a wonderful camp that has made a difference in our daughter's life, regards."

John Ahlfors, father of Tiffany Ahlfors, RYLA 1999

"Camp RYLA is this utopianish, talent enhancing, leadership-teaching, building experience that takes place every year in June. Starting as a camper in 1992, A.C. 1993, Staff 1994-1997 and Assistant Camp Director 1998-1999, I have seen and become acquainted with over 800 RYLArians. I have seen campers come in on the first day of camp, innocent and unsuspecting 11th graders, skeptical and inhibited. From Day 1, the campers are placed in the center of attention, showered with compliments, overwhelmed with positive peer pressure, and given the opportunity to dream. As a RYLArian, I had the opportunity to set goals — some of which I have already accomplished and some to which I still aspire. The biggest lessons that I have learned are about love and service. A person who knows love is willing to give and serve without the expectation of compensation. Thank you, Mark, for being that "special somebody" to me.

Blanca Espinosa, RYLArian, AC, Staff and Asst. Camp Director

4

WOMEN IN ROTARY

Women in Rotary, you ask? Banish the thought. Absurd. Are you kidding? These were some of the remarks making the rounds of Rotary clubs during the middle 80's. For many years, there had been a women's "auxiliary", called Rotary Anns or Rotary Inner Wheel. When the subject of women in Rotary came up in any group discussion, everyone seemed to have his/her own opinions, and nobody seemed to be on the fence. You were either "fer" or "agin" it. Although I was never part of a poll, my observation seemed to be that it was about 25% "fer" and 75% "agin".

My own rationale as one of the minorities was that Rose and I had three daughters and a son: that each of the daughters was a business or professional woman, but that it didn't really make that much difference in our family, since none of the daughters had ever expressed a desire to get into Rotary...and probably wouldn't. That changed. In 1990, while I was serving as district governor, my middle daughter, Diane, joined the Addison (TX) Rotary Club. She is presently president of the Golden, Colorado Rotary Club and will be serving as an Assistant Governor in District 5450 for the 1999-2000 year.

One of the many requirements that Rotary International specifies for a Rotarian to be nominated for district governor is that the member have been in Rotary for a minimum of seven years. The first Rotary year that any female Rotarian could be elected was the 1995-1996 year. Out of the 504 districts in the world, only eight women Rotarians were elected by their districts to serve that year. One of the eight was Janet Holland (classification Retail Hardware) of Mineral Wells, TX in District 5790.

Janet joined Rotary in 1988. She served as president of the Mineral Wells Club in 1992. In addition to having been District Governor, she has served Rotary International in many capacities, including Vice-Chairman of Women in Rotary Committee, Team Leader of the Carl P. Miller Discovery Grant to Bangladesh in 1997, and Rotary President's Golden Citation Awards in 1996 and 1997.

Janet Holland, District 5790 (North Central Texas)

"Some of the earliest memories of my life were of Rotary. However, I didn't realize what Rotary was at the time. I remember going to many meetings with my parents, where there were very few children, and much of the time I was admonished to "behave myself." I was four years old when my father, W. Lee Woodward, was Rotary Governor of District 124 (now Districts 5750 and 5770) in Oklahoma. Whenever we traveled, the first thing my mother did was to pull out the Official Directory from under the front seat of the car where it always stayed. It was a challenge to see how many Rotary clubs my father could attend on each trip. We would speed up, slow down and go out of our way to make a meeting. I didn't realize we were different. I thought all families traveled that way!

As I was growing up, frequent visitors in our home were men who had been district governors about the same time as my father. Some of them served as RI directors and one, J. Edd McLaughlin from Ralls, Texas, was RI president in 1960-61. It seemed as though I had always been a Rotarian with so much of my life touched by Rotary. I didn't hesitate when I was asked to join, I was eager to become involved.

In 1989, I took Hugh Archer's theme "Enjoy Rotary" to heart by joining the International Skiing Fellowship of Rotarians. Those IFSR ski weekends introduced me to Rotarians beyond the district. Two years later, the fellowship decided that we needed to grow and get more Rotarians around the world involved in the ISFR. Because we own a hardware store, they decided that I must know marketing and public relations, so the task of publicity and membership fell to me. Imagine the excitement in our hardware store in rural Texas when I had phone calls from Rotarians in Turkey, New Zealand and Italy, all in a single day! This was my introduction to the international aspect of Rotary International. From 1993-95, as president of the ISFR, I was the first woman to head an international fellowship. That honor was overshadowed by the honor and pleasure of meeting with RI President Bob Barth in his Evanston office. At that time I presented him with two official pins of the skiing fellowship making President and Mrs. Barth honorary members of ISFR.

I was surprised when Rotarians began to ask if I would consider being nominated for district governor. My response was that Rotarians around the district probably didn't know me well enough. They convinced me that they all knew me as the Rotarian who attended a district conference on crutches, a result of my first ski fellowship week-end. And the conference was held on two floors of a resort that had no elevator!

Jumping from running a hardware store, with all its nuts and bolts, plumbing supplies, paint, etc. to the International Assembly was like going into another world. That week in Anaheim was an unbelievable experience. We made friends instantly, talked to and really got to know people from around the world, shared the common interest in Rotary and planned joint projects. How can you explain to anyone who has not been there what it means and how it changes your life? Having the opportunity to participate in that one week was worth all the work and time spent preparing for and being district governor. I would do it all again just for that week's experience in Anaheim.

I had wondered how we, the women who were governor nominees would be received by the other nominees, especially those from outside the USA. One of my fondest Anaheim memories was of a governor nominee from Thailand. He left no doubt in my mind how welcome we were. When I met him one day in the lobby, he was so disappointed that he hadn't brought his camera. He wanted his picture taken with one of the women nominees. The next day we saw each other at the same time and place in the lobby as though it were planned. He had his camera and was very pleased to see me again. As we were posing for the picture, I looked up and saw two other women nominees getting out of the elevator.

By the time the picture was taken, he had two women nominees on each side of him. Four of us surrounding the Thai nominee! Everywhere we went, people wanted pictures of the first women nominees and a chance to get to know us.

Looking back at the year I spent preparing to be governor, it seems like a blur. At the time, I thought I was very well organized. I had told our daughter, Michele, and our son, Daniel, that they could marry anytime they wanted, except from January, 1995 until July, 1996, when my time would be filled with preparing for and being governor. That was a mistake! I should never have mentioned marriage. Both of them, ages 29 and 27, decided to marry and their weddings would be during the first two months of my year as governor. Our daughter was in a doctoral program in west Texas but wanted to marry in her home church and have the reception at home, so I did most of the work after she made the decisions about her wedding. RI President Herb Brown was stressing the importance of family, so I put my family first and didn't start my club visits until July 18th, three days after her wedding. Daniel's wedding was in August. Although I was not as involved in his wedding, it was still a very busy time juggling the wedding activities with my Rotary responsibilities.

In addition to the week in Anaheim, some of my best memories of the year are of the club visits. During the second week of my visits, Arlington Sunrise Rotarians took me to see some of their club projects, including playground equipment they and the community had built when they were a very young club. When we returned to my hotel, I was speechless when I looked up and saw the marquee "Welcome Rotary District Governor Janet Holland" It suddenly struck me that I was IT! I really was "GOVERNOR." After a year and a half of preparation, the time had come.

During the third week of the visits, I went to Vernon, a club of 55 men. The only thing they would talk about at the club assembly was how to get women members and not lose the members they had. Whatever we were discussing, women members came up again. In closing, I told them I would come back to induct their first woman member. A month later they called me to come to induct their first *five* women and also five men!

I stepped into the role of governor in an already active and enthusiastic district. The outstanding leadership in our district during the previous years had established a strong foundation of service and programs, on which we were able to build. The past governors' help was always willingly given whenever I asked. We have been extremely involved in matching grants, which has led to other international interest and projects. District Rotarians are now looking for projects as they travel. One Rotarian, while giving a banking seminar in Mongolia and visiting the new Rotary club there, learned of their desire to start the first English language library in the country. Upon his return, his club began collecting "Books for Mongolia." When others in the district learned of the project, they wanted to participate, so we adopted it as a district project. Of the 42,000 pounds of books collected, one of our provisional clubs contributed over 12,000 pounds of that total.

My year as governor ended when I served as chairman of the Texas Breakfast at the Calgary Convention. It was a time of celebration, meeting new friends, renewing friendships with Rotarians from around the world and making promises to meet again. There's no better way to end a once-in-a-lifetime experience than that.

July 1, 1996, arrived and the calendar told me the year as governor was over. Although most of our goals were met or surpassed, not all our projects were completed. As a result of our outstanding Group Study Exchange with Bangladesh, we have applied for our first Carl Miller Discovery Grant to help the Rotary Club of Jabalabad, Sylhet, Bangladesh, in establishing the country's first rehabilitation hospital. Their team leader, Dr. Monzur Choudhury, visited a rehabilitation hospital while in our district. He went home dreaming of establishing one for the people in his area. His club adopted his dream, prompting him to write us asking for our assistance by using the Discovery Grant.

In the spring of 1997, The Rotary Foundation approved our grant application for travel of Charles Wilson, a physical therapist, and me to Sylhet. Because of that grant, the Rotarian dream of establishing the Jalalabad Disabled Rehabilitation Centre and Hospital is becoming a reality. The Rotary Club of Jalalabad and our District 5790 are working together to make it possible. The 39 members of the Jalalabad Club have raised the money and built a multi-storied building to house the hospital and clinic. We advise them when asked, encourage them and spread the word about this undertaking to Rotarians and others whenever possible. We are partnering with them on matching grants for the latest rehabilitation equipment.

The Rotary Club of San Francisco West took charge of equipment donated by a Shriner's Hospital in their area when they closed their facility. The 14 members catalogued, repaired, and stored the donated equipment to be shipped to the Jalalabad Rehabilitation Centre. That equipment is now in place. We will be helping to arrange for volunteer physical therapists to be at the Centre for several years. Speech and occupational therapists will also be needed. Ultimately, the goal is to establish a school to train and license Bangladeshi students as therapists. Even years from now, volunteers will be needed for continuing education and to bring the newest methods of rehabilitation to their staff. Our support of the Centre is, and will be, on-going.

The Centre is an outstanding example of the Rotary Foundation's goal of achieving better world understanding and peace through service to humanity. As more Rotarians become involved in this project through contributions and as volunteers, it will become a world-wide project. The benefits to the people of Sylhet area and throughout Bengladesh are unlimited and timeless. Without Rotary, Rotarians and The Rotary Foundation, this project would not have been possible. If anyone has ever wondered if one person can make a difference, he needs only to be involved in a project such as this one. One person's idea and each individual working to carry out that idea is what makes things happen. I am so thankful that I have had the opportunity to be a Rotarian and to be a very small part of all that is being done to make the world a better place. Being a Rotarian has truly changed my life!

5

THE FOUR-WAY TEST

Stephen H. Miller

Steve joined the Rotary Club of Dallas in 1984, with the classification of "Attorney". In 1992, he became a member of Park Cities Rotary Club, under the classification of "Criminal Law". In order to be closer to his law office, he changed his membership to Plano Rotary Club during 1997. He has served enthusiastically as District 5810 Four-Way Test Speech Chairperson for five of the last six years. Here is his story:

Everyone who becomes a Rotarian eventually learns the story behind the Four-Way Test penned by Herbert J. Taylor in 1932. In the midst of the Great Depression, Mr. Taylor left his position as Executive Vice President of Jewel Tea Company in 1930 at the request of a Vice-President of Continental National Bank in Chicago to try to keep the Club Aluminum Products Company from declaration of bankruptcy. Borrowing $6,100 against his Jewel Tea stock, he accepted a position as President of Club Aluminum Products Company at a salary of $6,000 a year. The 250 employees of the company and their families were dependant upon Taylor's leadership to bring the company back from a $400,000 debt.

However, it wasn't Mr. Taylor's leadership that saved Club Aluminum Products Company. It was his faith in God. His first task was to set policies for the company that would reflect the high ethics and morals God would want in any business. With divine inspiration, Mr. Taylor recorded the twenty-five words that have come to be known as the Four-Way Test.

1. Is it the truth?

2. Is it fair to all concerned?

3. Will it build good will and better friendships?

4. Will it be beneficial to all concerned?

Mr. Taylor called it "The Four-Way Test" of the things we think, say or do.

Within five years, the $400,000 debt of the Club Aluminum Products Company was paid in full. During the next 15 years, the company distributed over one million dollars in stock dividends and the net worth of the company climbed to over $1,750,000.00. The original $6,100 which Mr. Taylor had pledged against his Jewel Tea stock was the only money the company had borrowed or invested in that miraculous twenty-year span.

In 1942 Rotary International was given the right to use The Four-Way Test. A member of the Board of Directors of Rotary International had asked for permission to use the test to promote Rotary's objectives of high ethical standards.

In January, 1954, Mr. Taylor was chosen to become president of Rotary International, for its great Golden Anniversary year of 1955. He unselfishly presented the copyright for the Four-Way Test to Rotary International, while retaining the right to use it for himself, Club Aluminum Products Company and the Christian Workers Foundation.

The world is certainly a better place because of Herbert J. Taylor. Any person who pauses to check his thoughts, words or actions against The Four-Way Test before speaking or acting is certain to do the right thing. The earlier young people apply the test, the earlier they will begin to realize their true potential in whatever path they take in life.

There are many activities in Rotary District 5810 that are designed to benefit young adults. Those programs include Camp Enterprise, RYLA, D.F.Y.I.T., Rotary Youth Exchange, Ambassadorial Scholarships, Interact, Career Days, and others. However, in my opinion, there is no program better designed to communicate the ethical guidelines by which all Rotarians strive to live by than the Four-Way Test Speech Contest.

To introduce young people to Rotary's Four-Way Test, our district began sponsoring a speech contest for high school students. Most of the students are selected for the competition by debate coaches or speech teachers. Of those who compete, I find that most of them have had no previous exposure to Rotary. They are given copies of the Four-Way Test and are asked to develop a 5-7 minutes presentation, based on their interpretation of "The Test" as it applies to their everyday life.

Most of the Rotary Clubs in our district participate in the program. Each club invites four or five students from their neighborhood high school to compete in a club contest. They attend a regularly scheduled club meeting to make his/her presentation. Clubs continue to report that the level of all presentations is excellent and that it is difficult to select winners. Plaques and/or cash awards are presented to the winners, who are generally selected by a team of non-Rotarians.

Each club winner then is asked to attend a district-wide competition. Winners are determined on a 1, 2, 3 basis (with cash awards), and the overall winner is asked to make his/her presentation at the next District Conference.

It is hoped that during this experience, each contestant will become more familiar with Rotary, and will express a desire to become a Rotarian after their formal education is complete and they have established themselves in a career or vocation.

6

POLIO PLUS

It has been referred to on many occasions as "Rotary's Finest Hour" .....and with good reason. What started as a vision or dream of a small group of Rotarians became one of the greatest humanitarian programs ever implemented by *any* organization. It started simply as "Polio" and when it blossomed, became "PolioPlus." One of the dedicated Rotarians who became involved during the early stages of the program was PDG Ray Kneggs. Ray has been a member of the Garland (TX) Lakeside Club since 1974, served as its president in 1977-78, and District Governor, 1984-85. He has served Rotary International as National Coordinator for Polio Plus from 1986-1988, Foundation Permanent Fund Advisor, 1997, and was the recipient of the prestigious Rotary International Service Above Self award in 1998.

PDG Ray Kneggs, District 5810

I received a telephone call early one morning in October, 1985, from Past International Director Jack Forrest, asking me if I could be in Evanston by 4 P.M. that afternoon for a very important meeting about a new Rotary International program. Jack did not say what it was about, but I knew Jack well enough that he would not have called that early if it were not important. I made it.

He had called together 25 Rotarians to serve as National Coordinators for a program that was being undertaken to eradicate Polio from the face of the earth by the year 2000.

In 1984-85, the President of Rotary International was Dr. Carlos Canseco, Jr. from Monterrey, Mexico. He had as his theme for the year, "Discover a New World of Service." It was because of his vision that we implemented what is now referred to as "PolioPlus.".

At Rotary's 1985 International Convention in Kansas City, the inventor of the great vaccine drops, Dr. Albert Sabin, spoke about the urgent need to develop a world-wide polio immunization program. When Dr. Canseco mentioned to Dr. Sabin that he thought it would take Rotary ten years to raise enough funds for a meaningful program, Dr. Sabin's response was, "We can't wait ten years!" At this convention, a goal was set of $120,000,000 to be raised during the next three years.

I shall never forget when we arrived at the International Convention in Philadelphia three years later. During the opening of the convention, the excitement created by giant fire cracker and flash lighting displays was electrifying, and told us that the goal had not only been reached....it had doubled to $240,000.000.

Rotary was then ready to start implementing the program. Herbert A. Pigman, former General Secretary of Rotary International, was named General Coordinator.

One of the great problems that we faced was getting the vaccine to the point of administering it to the children. Such was the case in Mexico, where over 12 million children were immunized in one day! This was achieved when a Rotarian of a company with refrigerated trucks donated the use of 16 of them for that day of immunization. The process has been repeated many times in Africa, India, Philippines, Brazil and all over the world. At the scene, local health authorities, along with many of our Rotarians who are medical professionals, assisted the local health officials with the immunizations.

I would like to share with you some of the personal experiences that I was privileged to participate in with this program. In Delhi, India, on a Sunday morning at 6 am., all of the Rotarians and local health professionals were mobilized for a national day of immunization. We picked up the vacinne at the hospital and proceeded to eight locations, which had been set up for the immunization. The unsanitary conditions that we saw as we proceeded through the city were indescribable. As we saw the sparsely clothed, under-nourished children, we wondered "What do they really have to look forward to?"

The fourth location for the day was a school yard. There was a brick wall around the school, with loose bricks, debris, open doors with no window covers, with one desk sitting out in the middle of the court yard, where the nurse sat ready for the immunizations. As I looked up I saw two young children coming through the gate. One was a young boy about ten years of age, leading his sister by the hand; she was about four years old. As they approached, I noted an expression on the face of the girl which I interpreted as fear or wonderment of what she was about to have done to her.

With big brother standing by her side, I asked her to open her mouth. She did not understand what I said, so her brother told her in Hindi to do so; she did and I dropped two drops on her tongue. That was it. As they left, I realized that the Polio program was really working -- one person at a time.

We were somewhat astounded to realize that when the campaign started, 40% of the known polio cases were in India alone! Some 22 million dollars was originally allocated to address this problem in India. Some of the other major challenges of the world are to serve the Philippines, Brazil, and many countries in Africa.

In 1995, the trustees of the Rotary Foundation decided that we must initiate a new program, whereby districts could use some of their available funds for matching grants to fund some of these special projects in different parts of the world. This is called PolioPlus Partners. The Matching Grant program of The Rotary Foundation make matching funds available to support immunization in particularly needy districts in the world.

We are well on our way toward reaching our original goal, but there is still a lot of work to do be done before it is completed.

Of all the Rotary projects in which I have been privileged to be a part of on the club, district, and international level, I am most proud of my personal involvement in PolioPlus. The Plus part of this program is that the World Health Organization and UNICEF immunizes against the other major diseases, such as measles, tetanus, tuberculosis, etc., at the same time we do Polio.

I will always believe that this has been "Rotary's Finest Hour!"

7

GROUP STUDY EXCHANGE

Hugh B. McAfee, Jr.

Hugh joined the Space Center Rotary Club in 1970 before moving to Dallas in 1974, where he joined the Rotary Club of Park Cities. He served as president in 1987-88. In the spring of 1989, he was selected to be Team Leader of a Group Study Exchange team to District 264 in Japan.

Page 31 of Volume 7 of the Basic Rotary Library, THE ROTARY FOUNDATION, states that the objectives of the highly successful Group Study Exchange program are: (1) To provide outstanding young business and professional persons opportunities for observing another country, its people and institutions, through participation in an organized program of study and discussion. (2) To further international understanding by allowing persons of good will to meet, talk and live with each other in a spirit of fellowship, so that they may get to know each other's problems and aspirations, and permit such personal contacts to ripen into lasting friendships. (3) To involve Rotarians in a specific and practical International Service Project by organizing educational programs for Group Study Exchange teams and providing hospitality for them.

From many years of personal experience, I can attest to the fact that those lofty ideals become a reality over and over again throughout the Rotary world. My own involvement in GSE came about sometime in the spring of 1988 when D/581 Governor C. C. Collie gave me the opportunity to lead a team to D/264 in Japan. Five young men were selected in time for an in-depth training schedule, including a week of intensive Japanese language study. On March 17, 1989, when we flew out of Dallas for Osaka, we were a well-prepared and motivated cadre of ambassadors.

Because of typical Rotary plans and preparations, at both ends, the trip for all six of us was truly the experience of a lifetime. It fulfilled all of the ideals pronounced in the objectives of the program. We saw and experienced Japan as no tourist or business traveler could. Several of the team, including the leader, still communicate with friends that we met in Japan during that wonderful five week experience. The hospitality of the Japanese Rotarians was above and beyond expectations in every way.

That fantastic trip was only the beginning of many privileges and honors from GSE. I was involved as a GSE committee member or district chairman from 1989 until 1997, when we moved from Dallas. As chairman, I was able to experience the thrill of seeing bright young men and women have their lives changed by the GSE programs. This was true for both the outgoing teams and for the wonderful people we hosted from across the Rotary world -- people who are making a mark for society because of GSE.

During those eight years from 1989 to 1997, we exchanged with Australia, Japan, New Zealand, Sweden, Mexico, Canada, India, Brazil, Germany and the Philippines. In each case the outgoing teams came home with wonderful tales of great experiences, and the incoming teams quickly became our cherished friends....friends we might never have known without GSE.

Some incidents from each side of the equation stick in my mind to illustrate the great experiences for these young travelers. One young woman on the trip to Sweden had graduated from the University of Texas with a degree in Exercise Physiology. During her Vocational week in Sweden, she spent a day with the author of one of her major text books. A young police sergeant from Garland was able to exchange ideas and experiences with a high official of the Royal Canadian Mounted Police in Vancouver.

A merchandise controller from the J. C. Penney company had lunch with the chairman of the board of Japan's largest department store chain. An architect and his landscape architectural team leader were able to spend a day studying the Taj Mahal in India.

From the incoming teams the stories are equally as heart-warming. One in particular tells it all. We had to do some heavy duty selling to persuade the Bonham, TX club to host the team from Mexico. It was the club's first experience and they were fearful. The only problem came when we went to move the young Mexican team from Bonham to the next club. The Mexicans wanted to stay and the Bonham Rotarians didn't want to give them up!

An added bonus from the GSE program is the number of team members who accept invitations to become Rotarians soon after they return home. One of this group, Lynn Garison, a member of the team to New Zealand became a member of the Rotary Club of Park Cities and has just completed a very successful year as the first woman president of the second-largest club in D/5810. Lynn is a perfect example of a Rotary leader that can come from the GSE program.

Roger Pryor, Rotary Club of White Rock (Dallas) Texas

After having been in Rotary for 29 years, serving as president of the White Rock club in 1975, attending numerous district assemblies, conferences and two International Conventions, I thought I knew quite a bit about Rotary.....then I realized that I had more to learn...much more!

I knew a little bit about Rotary's Group Study Exchange program and had thought about making application to be Group Leader. After "threatening" on several occasions, I asked my club to sponsor me for team leader to Chile, which would be out-bound in April, 1998. I was delighted when I was selected in the fall of 1997.

The team was then selected: two men and two women. It was fortunate for the entire team that two had excellent bilingual skills, two had a good understanding of the language; and all had international travel experience.

I had never been to South America, but had studied Spanish in both high school and college. With our rapidly expanding markets in the Americas, I felt that this was a great opportunity to serve Rotary and at the same time enhance my knowledge of a different country and culture.

District 4320 in Northern Chile is the longest district in Rotary. It is over 1,250 miles in length and only about 80-110 miles wide. In our month long visit, we traveled almost 2,000 miles -- by bus, car, or truck. We attended 19 Rotary Club meetings and met with 24 Rotary Clubs (some were combined meetings). We also attended their three day District Conference and presented a forty minute program, all in Spanish!

We saw historical places, commercial ventures, marine life farms, the driest desert in the world -- the Atacama, the Andes, ancient ruins, beautiful coastal cities, and even a ski resort. But most of all, we met many, many dedicated Rotarians who individually and through their clubs are strongly committed to serve others. Truly, "Service Above Self" is in action in Chile.

Let me tell you something of what I learned about these caring, hard working, service-minded Rotarians in Northern Chile. One small club initiated a service project to surgically correct cleft palates and lips in young people. This project expanded from one club to several clubs in the District to the whole of Chile -- four districts! Another club, on the Argentine border, helped to negotiate a peace agreement with Argentina through an Argentine Rotary club. Yet another small club in the District paid for and built a community center that houses the fire department and provides space for community activities. A large club has begun a program to provide, free of charge, pace makers to Chileans who have Chagas disease and who otherwise would die.

Everywhere we went, the comment was the same. "You (North Americans) have the money, we have the needs." No pretense or resentfulness -- simply an objective comment with much truth to it. No apologies nor begging. "We have a need; you can help us financially or in procuring assistance, resources, and personnel." The money and volunteer medical professionals for the cleft palate surgeries are from the U.S.

As we visited the clubs, we found that the spirit of service and the goals of Paul Harris were everywhere. Rotary, new to Chile? Hardly. The first club was established in Chile in 1924 and nine of the clubs we visited were founded more than 70 years ago. Most clubs are small, with twenty-five members or less; they meet at night from 9 PM to midnight. They are all seeking ways to help their communities.

Neither my life nor my commitment to Rotary will ever be the same. There is much to live for and endless opportunities for us to serve those around us. For me, my Group Study Exchange experience has opened my eyes and heart to promote and be involved in "SERVICE ABOVE SELF."

PDG Milton Kessel

In another chapter of this book, as part of stories on RYLA (Rotary Youth Leadership Awards), it was mentioned that I had served as the Group Study Exchange leader of an all-women's team to Rotary District 960, Queensland, Australia, in the spring of 1989. While there, I learned about the wonderful RYLA program, which originated in Australia in the middle 60's.

There were so many pleasurable moments and experiences during that visit that to mention just one or two occasions simply wouldn't do justice to the five, fun-filled weeks spent in "the land down under."

Texans have the reputation of being friendly. But at the expense of making what sounds like (and is) a "class" statement, the Aussies are, by inherent nature, not only friendly, but possess all of the other attributes of the Boy Scouts....courteous, kind, cheerful, trustworthy, loyal, helpful, et al. What a great bunch of people!

Since our district had selected an all-women team of members, Rotary International required both the Rotarian and spouse to accompany the GSE team. This presented absolutely no problem to Rose!

Although our experiences in home hosting were all outstanding and most pleasurable, we would like to make special mention of two of our eight, great host families.

Each member of a GSE team, including the leader, looks forward to the "vocational week" of their visit, during which time the member is hosted by a Rotarian who is in the same profession or business as the participant. This is intended as a means of both the host and guest learning more about the trade practices and customs of the other's country.

Our host family during that week was Glen and Heather Kinross of the Hamilton Rotary Club. Glen was a manufacturer of contemporary dining room furniture. I had within the year sold my retail furniture stores and was then on the staff of Home Furnishings International Association.

They lived in Wavell Heights, Queensland, a small community near Brisbane. Glen had served Rotary in many capacities, including International Director and Vice-President in 1983-84. Glen not only got me acquainted with all phases of his own manufacturing business, but made sure that I visited a number of retail stores in the area, to show me, first-hand, how furniture was marketed in Australia. His wife, Heather, was a gracious host to us both. Eight years after our GSE visit to District 960, in July, 1997, Glen became the President of Rotary International. We were so pleased during his year as president that he and Heather were present at our Texas PETS program and we had a great opportunity to renew acquaintances. Rose and I were deeply saddened, however, when shortly after a year of world travel with Glen as the First Lady of Rotary, Heather Kinross passed away.

Our second host family during the visit was Rose and Ian Craig. Ian had been owner of a hardware company in Burpengary, a small community in Queensland. They had recently sold their business to their son, built a new home, and Ian was in the first year of retirement.

The long hallway in their new home was lined with pictures of young teenagers, and when we asked them if they were their grandchildren, they replied, "well, yes, in a way....they are the foreign exchange students whom we have hosted over the past 20 years." They had their first student in 1969, and as of this writing, have had 15, from most parts of the Rotary world. Their home has become an "International House", as many of the students have returned to visit them and the student's parents and siblings have also stayed with them during visits. Rose Craig talks proudly of her five American "grandchildren" and has *visited them all!*

While on one of their trips to the United States in 1990, we had the pleasure of having the Craigs in our home. After ten years, the two Roses (Craig and Kessel) correspond at least once a quarter. They have a lot to write about. What a great international friendship!

Rotary is replete with outstanding business and professional executives, in all trades and professions. One of these is William E. (Bill) Sleeper, past president of the Park Cities (Dallas) TX Rotary Club. He is president and CEO of Sleeper, Sewell & Company, a multiple-line insurance agency. The company serves commercial and personal clients in property, casualty, life and health insurance. His expertise is in risk management consulting, in analysis, transfer funding and risk control. He currently serves as national president of the 28,000 member CPCU (Chartered Property & Casualty Underwriters) organization.

During the early part of the 1996 Rotary year, Bill was selected to be the team leader for Rotary's Group Study Exchange team from District 5810 to Bavaria, Germany (District 1840). Here is an interesting account of the GSE visit to Germany.

William E. (Bill) Sleeper

It wasn't as if I knew little about Rotary. I knew, for example that the Rotary International Foundation helped people. I knew it felt good to participate. And it wasn't that I didn't know that The Rotary Foundation supported GSE (although I didn't know the full extent). My father had been a GSE leader to Brazil and he told of heartwarming friendships, terrific parties and a warm relationship with the men he led on that trip.

Dad told a story about being the victim of a mugging in Brazil. The perpetrators were pretty clever. They grabbed him, obviously the oldest and most prosperous of the five, in a vulnerable part of his body. When he tried to protect himself, an accomplice picked his pocket. A total of about US$50 was taken. But let me tell you, the story got better and better each time it was re-told, and the $50 lost was a small price to pay for the comedy material.

Fast-forward a decade. My wife and I liked Germany and were determined to go there for a 1996 summer vacation. My daughter was there with her Air Force dentist husband, and we were excited about seeing them. It was announced that the Rotary district was seeking applications for a team leader to Germany. So, "I gave it a shot." I was fortunate enough to have been selected, and although I was to be gone for five weeks, was pleased to get the encouragement of my wife, Mica, as well as my business associates. Incidentally, Mica worked out a trip to Germany with a neighbor friend while I was gone, and one afternoon we crossed paths in Bavaria for a brief visit.

It was well before we left for Germany that the spirit of the program came to me. As leader, it was my job to form a team. I participated in the selection process. One of the points which we had to pass along to all member applicants was that *this was not a vacation,* that in effect, all of the team members were ambassadors of their country and their mission was to present their professions or vocations in their best manner, and to benefit from their experiences while in Germany, particularly related to their own field of work.

The preparation itself entailed twelve meetings to prepare our presentation to the German clubs, our understanding of Rotary (the team members were not Rotarians) and to develop our knowledge of the country and as much as we could, of their language.

Why would Rotary International spend the money to send us to Europe? The answer came to me clearly as we got into our club visits in Germany. It was in relationships. First, it was the relationship of our members to one another. I think we genuinely appreciated each other.

More importantly, it was the friendships we made with our wonderful hosts and Rotary friends. Here's an illustration. One of the team members, Darrick Eugene, grew up in one of the rougher neighborhoods in Houston, Texas. In spite of his early environment, he excelled in school and earned a Masters in Public Administration. When he applied for the exchange, he was a department manager of AT&T in Dallas. One day early in our trip, with a large tear running down his cheek, he told me that he had to go home because of a serious illness in his family. Mr. Forster, the host parent, made arrangements to take Darrick to the airport to return to Texas.

Fortunately, ten days later Darrick was able to return to the team and we were delighted. In the meantime, Mr. Forster's father-in-law passed away. When Derrick returned, the Forsters welcomed him back into their family, which had gathered for the funeral. He became a member of the family, despite being an African-American who didn't resemble his new family at all. The emotional ties that were formed were unimaginable and these warm relationships will remain forever in Darrick's heart. We were all friends invited into their homes, not tourists in a crowd. This is Group Study Exchange!

GSE is people and experiences. Like when Herr Mengle took me to the bandstand so I could lead the band at the volksfest while our team and new friends could cheer and clap. Like when my shoe became radioactive in the nuclear power plant and is now consigned to a waste dump in Europe. I still love my German replacement shoes.

During our first Sunday in the biergarten, a man old enough to have served in the German military told me with a smile and rough English that his experience in Louisiana in a prisoner of war camp brought pleasant memories of America!

After we returned, our team completed its requisite report. In it were each member's recollections, highlights, advice, and expressions of sincere appreciation for the experience. My cover letter addressed the questions, "Did we meet the goals of the Group Study Exchange?" Indeed we did, especially in connection with world peace and understanding. I am proud of the friendships we formed. We thoroughly related to our wonderful hosts and soaked up the culture and environment. The beautiful churches, innovative businesses, historic sites, incomparable scenery, sumptuous restaurants, delightful parties were all memorable. Nothing to me was more precious, though, than the sheer pleasure of the company of friends. The laughter, the joking and the friendships, were the extraordinary part of the trip. *All of us wish we could go again!"*

8

AMBASSADORIAL SCHOLARSHIPS

'The Rotary Foundation Ambassadorial Scholarship program is the world's largest privately funded international scholarship program. In 1947, 18 "Rotary Fellows" from 13 countries were selected to serve as ambassadors of goodwill while studying in another country for one academic year. Since that time, approximately US$335 million has been expended on some 30,000 scholarships for people from 125 countries, studying in 105 countries around the world."

....from The ABCs of Rotary

It is almost superfluous to refer to a Rotary Ambassadorial Scholar as being "outstanding", because in order to have been selected from so many highly qualified applicants for the Award, that person would possess outstanding traits of knowledge, leadership and direction.

One such Scholar is Julie Groschen Richey, of Irving, Texas. Julie attended the University of Dallas, graduated in 1987, and was awarded her Rotary scholarship to Italy 1987-88, where she took her graduate study of Art History in Perugia, Italy. Julie returned to Dallas in June, 1988, worked in a commercial art gallery, then as Community Relations Manager for the Irving Arts Center, later as Associate Director of the Dallas Business Committee for the Arts, and finally as Public Relations Director at the Volunteer Center of Dallas County, before *retiring* to raise two daughters.

Julie Groschen Richey

The director of the prestigious Uffizi Gallery in Florence; the co-owner of a high-fashion Italian clothing company; the proprietor of a beautiful hotel which sits right on the banks of the Arno River in Florence; an Italian photographer who is a credit to his *papparuzzi* colleagues: What do these four men have in common, besides the fact that they reside in one of the most treasured cities in Europe? They all are here to discover what Dallas does best---for it is the spring of 1991, and Dallas is on a quest to become a World Cup venue. These gentlemen are members of the World Cup committee, one which selects game sites in advance of the world's most anticipated international sporting event.

Oh, and they have one more thing in common. This morning they are all crammed inside the tiny convertible I am driving from downtown Dallas to the Kimbell Art Museum in Ft. Worth. On a rainy Monday! Everyone knows that museums are closed Mondays. Even in Italy. But I carry precious cargo, and so a special, private tour has been arranged for us.

I grip the wheel, turn up the windshield wipers, search for the Italian equivalent of "Metroplex" and pray for safe passage. How did I get here? I asked myself this question several times over the week-long period of their visit. I wondered the same thing the previous evening, as I was seated between Dallas' Ambassador James Bullington and the Italian hotelier, pondering which of the four forks to use for my salmon carpaccio. My role at the dinner was strictly one of service---I was one of several Italian interpreters. I considered it a privilege to use the language skills I acquired during my year as a Rotary Foundation Scholar. As an added benefit, I was sitting amongst some of the finest 20th Century sculpture ever made, at the home of Raymond Nasher.

In 1987, I was sponsored by the Irving Rotary Club of District 581 to spend a year studying arts history in Perugia, Italy. Although I experienced the most intensely enriching year of my life traveling around Italy, France and Yugoslavia, some of the most rewarding work lay ahead, upon my return to Dallas.

One of the requirements of a Foundation Scholar is that upon his/her return from a year of study, a scholar must visit area Rotary clubs and speak about his/her experiences. My first speech was intimidating. Stand up in front of 75 strangers and give them the equivalent of Cliff's Notes to my epic year of study and travel? Where do I start? With the jovial and hospitable Rotary Host Counselor, who invited me to his home, and took me out for pizza with his family, and set up my bank account when no bank would allow foreign account holders? Or with the soaring Gothic churchesand monasteries we visited while on a school-sponsored trip to France? Or perhaps I should tell them about the people I met in Venice, young artists from many countries who came together by invitation to exhibit their cutting-edge artwork at Venice's Biennale, an international art exhibition held every two years. Would they believe my stories about the eccentric Venetian count who liked to appear in costume whenever he went out? Or the tale about the old monk on the Venetian cemetery island of San Michele, who showed me a private family's mausoleum and begged me to bring back some American corporate sponsorship to save his crumbling mosaics? How could I describe the time I was invited to spend the night with an Italian schoolmate's family? We ate homemade pasta with *vodka* in the sauce; we slept in her family's "guest room", a true Medieval tower overlooking the Umbrian countryside.

Now, more than ten years later, I don't remember much of that speech. I traveled with Rotarian Milton Kessel to virtually every club in the district. I even began to recognize members who were "making-up" missed meetings at other clubs. My many presentations did help me to understand that my audience of Rotarians was not composed of "strangers." They were more like uncles, aunts, neighbors, and even good friends. They supported my ambitions, reveled in my accomplishments, and wished me well. Each speech became easier, and my understanding of the principles behind Rotary International grew deeper.

I took Rotary's motto of "service above self" to heart, and was able to assist my community in several ways, thanks to the unique opportunity afforded to me by the Foundation Scholarship. One of my first jobs upon my return in 1988 was as Manager of Community Relations for the Irving Arts Center, a public facility which houses an art gallery, meeting rooms, performance halls and sculpture gardens. The City of Irving was in the process of forming a sister-city relationship with Marino, Italy, and I was asked to serve as an interpreter for a two-week trip to Marino and Rome. The purpose of the visit was "official," but Italians always have a way of turning everything into a festival. The friendships established on that visit continued, as the Italians made a reciprocal visit. Again, I was an interpreter for speeches, conferences, tours and dinners. Many members of the Irving Rotary club were also key in the establishment of the sister-city relationship. I was pleased to serve as an interpreter, which in some way allowed me to repay the generosity of the community which originally sponsored me.

Later, I took a job with the Dallas Business Committee for the Arts, and it was there that I was called to serve as an interpreter for the World Cup Committee visit. Dallas did eventually host several World Cup games, and I signed on as a Media Center interpreter during the games at Fair Park. I look back at my experiences, both in Italy as a Foundation Scholar and afterward in Dallas, and I see a common thread. Service, a word so integral to the Rotary International motto, has been a pleasure and a privilege for me.

I am very grateful for the opportunities to serve my community, and for the generosity of vision all Rotarians seem to hold in common. I do plan someday to be an active member of a Rotary Club, to do my part in ensuring the future of this invaluable scholarship program.

One of the early recipients of The Rotary Foundation's Scholarships was Neil. D. Anderson, who was sponsored by the Rotary Club of Dallas, Texas. Neil graduated from Rice University in 1960, and was the recipient of the Scholarship Award to The University of Brussels in the 1960-61 Rotary year. He received his law degree from Harvard University in 1964, and joined the Rotary Club of Dallas in 1967.

Neil D. Anderson

Opportunities come in many forms. One of my great opportunities came in the form of a Rotary International Fellowship. I had never heard of this fellowship but I was aware of the Rhodes, Marshall and Fullbright scholarships. Toward the end of my junior year, I asked about what scholarships might be available and was advised to apply for the Rotary award.

I knew a little about Rotary, since I had been the guest of the Dallas Rotary club while I was a high school student, so I applied. When word came of my award, I was pleased that I would be spending my year at the University of Brussels in Belgium.

The first indication I received of the true dimension of the Fellowship came the following summer. I was searching for a job in Europe that summer in order to acclimate myself to the new environment. I had written to the District Governor of Rotary in Belgium to inquire about opportunities of this nature that might be available. This would afford me an opportunity for direct contacts with Rotarians in the country in which I would study.

In the meantime, I secured a job in Paris. Subsequently, I had received a reply from the District Governor in Belgium, which was an offer for me to stay with three different Rotary families in Belgium for three weeks each during that summer. I was unable to accept because of my commitment to the position in Paris, but it was a portent of the hospitality that would be provided me during my stay in Belgium.

At the beginning of the school year in October, I journeyed from Paris to Brussels and was met at the train station by the daughter of the

District Governor with whom I had corresponded. His family welcomed me into their home and were my hosts and mentors throughout my stay in Brussels. I enrolled in the university and took up residence in one of the dormitories. I became an honorary member of the Rotary Club of Brussels -- Brussels had five Rotary clubs. In addition to attending the large Brussels club on a regular basis, I was invited to attend each of the other clubs in the city and speak concerning my homeland, my course of studies in Brussels and the Rotary International Fellowship.

Inasmuch as I planned on going to law school when I returned to the United States, I took courses in various aspects of the law at the University of Brussels, as well as other subjects that were of interest to me. I discovered that the Dean of the law faculty at the University, as well as one of my law professors, were members of the Brussels North Rotary Club. I was invited into the home of a number of Rotarians whom I had met at meetings, and through these invitations was able to participate in their life- style on a personal and meaningful basis. By visiting other Rotary clubs throughout Belgium, I was able to get to know the country and its inhabitants in a more profound manner. Typically, I would spend the night or a weekend with a host family and speak at a Rotary meeting.

I realized that Rotarians in Belgium represented the leaders in their community; I found that this was an especially insightful way to understand the contours of life in Belgium.

In addition to my studies and various Rotary visits, I traveled throughout western Europe and made a trip into what was then the Soviet Union. It had been explained that part of the stipend for my fellowship was to be used for travel as an educational augmentation to my studies.

When I returned to the United States and entered law school at Harvard University, the dean of the law school in welcoming remarks to the first year class mentioned those who had received various awards and introduced the Rhodes, Marshall, Fullbright recipients and Rotary fellows as a group. This confirmed for me the status of Rotary Fellowship as one of the most academically prestigious awards. But I also knew from my experience in Belgium that the Rotary Fellowship involved an extra dimension that was of immense value -- the contacts it provided from the fellowship with Rotarians.

The Fellowship became a life changing experience for me. It allowed me to encounter the larger world, to discover that other cultures have values and perspectives that are equally valid. It provided me with the confirmation that people of good will exist throughout other areas of the world, but it also provided me with a stronger realization of the worth of my own country.

I was very pleased when I returned to my home in Dallas to be invited to speak about my experiences to my home club, the Rotary Club of Dallas. I was glad to have the opportunity to tell them what they had provided me with through this Fellowship; for sometime thereafter, I thoroughly enjoyed the opportunity to speak to other clubs throughout the Rotary district. I wanted to communicate the message that Rotarians can be immensely proud of the program they support for foreign study through the Rotary Foundation.

I have now been a Rotarian for close to 30 years and have been involved in the district's scholarship activities for much of that time. I am pleased to do this because it give me some feeling of being able to return in a modest fashion what was so significantly provided for me through the Fellowship. I will always be grateful for this once-in-a-lifetime experience.

9

MATCHING GRANTS

"Among the many programs of The Rotary Foundation are the Matching Grants that assist Rotary clubs and districts in conducting International Service projects. Since 1965, more than 6,200 grants have been awarded for projects in about 165 countries, totaling more than US$56 million"

....from The ABC's of Rotary

PDG Conrad C. Heede, District 5790

Conrad Heede is a member and past president of the Grapevine, Texas Rotary Club, having joined Rotary in 1976. He served the district as Governor in 1991-1992. He is a Rotary Paul Harris Fellow, Benefactor, has been awarded The Rotary Foundation's Citation for Meritorious Service as well as the Distinguished Service Award. In 1998, he was awarded Rotary's prestigious Service Above Self Award. He has been instrumental in getting a number of The Rotary Foundation's Matching Grants for his district and tells how they have been arranged.

Anatomy of a Matching Grant

On the outskirts of Guadalajara there is a small mountain called Sierra del Quatro. For many years, no one built on this mountain because it was so steep and rocky. Then poor people from outlying areas moved to Guadalajara in the hope of finding jobs in the big city. Not being able to afford housing in the city, they built adobe huts on the slopes of the Sierra del Quatro. They had no roads, no electricity, no gas, no water, no sewers, and no city services at all. There were no schools and no way for the children to get to schools in other parts of the city. Without any chance of education, the children of these poorest of the poor families were destined to remain in poverty.

The Rotary Club of Guadalajara Ciudad del Sol, in conjunction with the church and other service organizations, decided to build a school near the top of the mountain. Since there were no level spots, they had to dig into the side of the mountain, eventually hauling off some 500 pick-up loads of dirt and rock, all dug by hand. They built the school, convinced some Catholic nuns to run it and found some teachers who would volunteer to make their way up the mountain every day to teach.

A social worker selected children from the poorest of the 20,000 families who lived there to attend the school. The children were excited to be going to school for the first time, but something unexpected happened. As excited as the children were every day, they would fall asleep about the middle of the morning. After some investigation, it was determined that the children had very little to eat that day, if anything at all. They didn't have enough calories in their bodies to stay awake all day.

The Rotarians then decided to feed the children. They acquired some used kitchen equipment and with donated food, mostly beans and rice, they were able to feed over 400 children the best meal they would have that day.

As the children progressed through school and were beginning to graduate, it was realized that few, if any of these children, would be going to the university. It was decided that they needed some vocational skills to make them more employable. Past President Alejandro Cortez invited me to see the school, with the idea that we would apply for a Matching Grant from The Rotary Foundation to provide some equipment to train the children in some traditional skills, such as wood and metal working, sewing, typing and pottery working. However, we decided to provide the school with computers, so that they could learn computer skills, which would enable them to get -- not just a job -- but a good job upon graduation....one that would break the cycle of poverty that their families had been in for generations.

We applied for two Matching Grants, one sponsored principally by the Weatherford Rotary Club, which supplied 15 computers and associated software. The other, sponsored principally by the Mineral Wells Rotary Club, supplied modern commercial kitchen equipment, so that better and more nutritious meals could be prepared. Thirteen clubs from Texas, from both D-5790 and D-5810, contributed 25% of the funding for these projects. Guadalajara cd del Sol contributed 25% and The Foundation matched the clubs' contributions.

Rotarians from many clubs have visited this school, and Rotarians from Guadalajara have visited many of our clubs as a result of these projects. A warm relationship has been developed among Rotarians from both countries. This has led, not only to many other humanitarian and educational projects, but also to the achievement of the Foundation's overall objective of world understanding and goodwill. Working together, we have given hope to the children and the families of the Sierra del Quatro, when they had no hope.

10

YOUTH EXCHANGE

"Youth Exchange is one of the most popular programs to promote international understanding and develop lifelong friendships. It began in 1927 with the Rotary Club of Nice, France. In 1939, an extensive Youth Exchange was created between California and Latin America. Since then the program has expanded around the world. In recent years more than 7,000 young people have participated annually in Rotary club and district-sponsored exchange programs."

....from the ABCs of Rotary.

Barbara Haynes

Barbara Haynes is an executive with GTE and holds the classification of "Telecommunications" in her Mid-Cities Pacesetters (Arlington, TX) Rotary Club. She was not a member of Rotary when she became involved with Rotary International's Youth Exchange program. Here is her story:

My name is Barbara Haynes. I am a single mom, mother of four daughters. Allison, my youngest daughter, is 15 1/2 years old, and is currently in Eschenbach, Germany with the Rotary International Exchange Program. Two of my other children have been Rotary Exchange students. It was the best experience in their lives to date, and it did more to prepare them for the future than any of the education and training they received in high school, college, law school, or graduate school.

In addition to my own children, this year I have been the host mother to Alona Gavrilova, a 16-year-old Russian Rotary Exchange student and Adryanno Pinheiro, a 16-year-old Brazilian exchange student from another exchange program.

Many people questioned my judgment in allowing Allison to exchange at such an early age, asking "How can you let your little girl go -- she is so young?" How can you put her on a plane to the unknown by herself?" Well, believe me, inwardly, I questioned myself. My questions, however, centered around how *I* was going to be able to live a whole year without her physical presence.

As parents we hopefully raise our children to be strong, independent, confident, secure individuals; we raise them to set goals and objectives and teach them to work hard at attaining those goals. We encourage them to live life to the fullest -- to live up to their own personal potential. Then, just when they exhibit this independence, this confidence, this sense of security, we selfishly wonder "How they can do this to us!"

For 10 years, Ali has had a dream - an objective and a goal - to one day be a Rotary International Exchange student. She began studying German in 5th grade. She attained excellent grades in all her subjects. Everything she had done for the past 10 years had been in preparation for this experience.

So, my response to these questioning friends is, "How could I not let her go?" This independent behavior is what I have strived so hard to accomplish in my parenting -- granted, she is exhibiting this independence a couple of years earlier than I had hoped -- but, I can't and I won't hold her back because I'm not ready.

Regardless of all this preparation on Ali's part and mine, the real answer to the question is very simple -- the confidence, the trust, the respect and the faith I have in the Rotary International Exchange program. You made this opportunity possible. She is living her dream, and you have prepared her well for this experience.

Let me now tell you a little bit about Alona, my Russian exchange student. Alona came to live with us in December. Alona savored every moment of life; as slowly as the days go by, it was too fast for her. She wanted to "taste" everything America had to offer.

Alona comes from a middle class family in Russia. Her parents are both university educated, and it was obvious that education and learning had been stressed in her family. But, as you know, middle class in Russia is very different from middle class here in the United States.

At first, Alona was very closed, very private and always very serious. She was the most practical, frugal child I have ever known. My little Russian was initially very fatalistic; she had a "nothing is possible" attitude. We had to prove everything over and over again. She looked at everything from the negative side and focused on why things would not work rather than on what it would take to make them work.

I explained to her that we would never introduce something to her if we didn't think there was a possibility of working it out. We would never "dangle a carrot" in front of her nose. Yet, she questioned. She would rather not dream, for fear of being disappointed.

Alona grew in so many ways in the last 10 months -- in more ways than I could ever have imagined. I am so thrilled that I was able to be a part of that growth -- to open her eyes to the possibilities in life. Alona has been a joy and inspiration to us, and to each of us in a very different way.

She understood her role as a Rotary exchange student; she understood her responsibility to the Rotary program, our family, and to her country. She was an excellent goodwill ambassador; she became a close friend, and I truly love her as a daughter.

As we were tearfully driving to the airport, she said, "At least I know now what is possible, and I know that *I* need to make it happen." She will never forget those who befriended her, for they gave her much more than they'll ever know; they gave her optimism and hope. She and I say, "Thank you!"

Let me now provide you with a completely different scenario. Imagine yourself in Brazil , a middle class family struggling to improve your child's opportunities for the future. Imagine the U.S. Embassy promoting foreign exchange programs.

You put your faith in the embassy's endorsement of a particular exchange program. You work 18 hours a day, 6 days a week for 2 years to save $7,000.00, the cost of the program, to provide this opportunity to your child. You fill out the application and send it off, along with your hard-earned money. There is no screening process; there is no interview process; there is no evaluation or selection process. You paid your money, your child goes. It matters not that, perhaps, your child is not mature enough to handle this experience, or that he understands his responsibility.

On August 24, 1994, your son boards a plane for the United States. Your dream has come true. There is no guaranteed host family, but you are assured that this is normal; that within just a few days, you will be given notification of a permanent family. Days pass, weeks pass -- still no permanent placement. The calls from him are more frequent now, and the self-assured kid no longer sounds confident and excited -- he just sounds scared.

After five weeks, your son is told by the temporary family that he will have to move -- that his host mother and father are separating and divorcing. He is told to <u>check around school</u> to see if anyone would be interested in hosting him. Your son tried repeatedly to contact his area rep, to no avail. Finally, after 6 weeks, the area rep. makes contact with your son -- she has found a permanent host family! With great relief and anticipation, your son travels to his new home. The family, single mother with one son, are away.

In all his life, your son has never seen such disarray and filth. He is devastated beyond imagination. The area rep explains "that this is a typical American home." Your son is upset and confused, but at least he now has a new home.

Several hours later, "the family" arrives home. The host mother welcomes your son into her home with a speech about how she had met the area rep at night school, and was keeping him as a favor to her. He was told that he would basically be on his own -- she works a lot, goes to school, and money is very tight.

There is no communication between the host brother and your son. He seems to resent the fact that your son is there, and your son certainly resents the fact that he has been placed there. This is America? The land of happiness, hope, prosperity and opportunity? Adryanno constantly wonders why he is here. His impressions of the United States, the American people and the "American Way" leave much to be desired.

My family met Adryanno on a Sunday afternoon in October, when Alona invited him and 11 other exchange students to our home to watch a Cowboy football game. He told us of his experiences to date, and how unhappy he was. He wanted very much to go home, but it would disgrace his family.

After he left our home, we discovered that he had left his sunglasses in the family room. The next evening, we returned them to him. There was no way I could be prepared for what I saw when I entered that home. How could a respected, supposedly conscientious youth exchange program allow this? How could they place a foreign student in such an environment? I was embarrassed for Adryanno; I was embarrassed for his program, and I was angry!

When Leanne and I arrived home, we discussed the situation with Allison. We all agreed, there was only one thing we could do -- we had no choice. I made a call to Mindy, the area rep.

Mindy *did* return my call. She was, of course, very defensive. She had no logical explanation for what had happened. Adryanno was dropped off on my doorstep the next evening, with an explanation that "It's very difficult to find good host families." As far as the program was concerned, and to quote his area rep, "Adryanno had been nothing but trouble since he arrived." How many more Mindy's are there in this program and in others like it that are only in it for profit and for the commission they receive for placing students? This program never screened; never evaluated their motivation, expectations, or their perception of their responsibility as an exchange student. They were never counseled; they never received any kind of orientation or guidance.

I have been asked to compare the Rotary program with some of the others with which I have had contact. There is no comparison!

No other program approaches the quality of Rotary's. It would be next to impossible for a Rotary student to experience what Adryanno experienced.

Please keep doing just exactly what you are doing -- the initial thorough application, the applicant screening, the interviewing and evaluating, the selection process, the mentoring, the counseling, the camp, the friendship and relationship building. As inbound counselors, be there when they need a friend, when they have doubts, when they have questions or concerns; be there when they need direction and help in resolving problems.

Thank you for giving me this opportunity to tell my story; thank you for the marvelous opportunity you have given my family and my little Russian daughter, Alona. And, thank you for giving me the confidence, the security and the trust in you to enable me to have the courage to send my daughter, Ali, off to live her dream.

You have made a very positive difference in our lives and the lives of many others. Rotarians should all be proud of this outstanding program!

It was on a Wednesday in the spring of 1983. I was "making up" at the Allen (TX) Rotary Club and took the opportunity to make an announcement about our up-coming annual Mini-Exchange in our district's Youth Exchange program with District 180 (the area around Hannover, West Germany). We had started the program with Germany back in 1980, when we were contacted by a Rotarian from Shoenegan, West Germany, who informed our governor that they would have up to twenty, young high school students who would be interested in coming to the United States for three weeks during the summer vacation period. In return, they would be pleased to host a like number of our students in Germany. The program was an instant success, and we were in the fourth year of the exchange.

During my announcement, I mentioned that the summer exchange had been set up basically for the benefit of sons and daughters of Rotarians, because many of Rotary's programs were not available to direct descendants of Rotarians.

There was a young lady sitting next to me who was the "student-of-the-month" from Allen High School. This club, as does many others, invites a high school senior to attend their meeting each week. She was Kris LaCroix, daughter of Ralph and Darlene LaCroix. Kris mentioned that her family was going to be hosting an Australian exchange student during the following school year, could she apply? She did, and was selected to go.

Since that occasion, the International Youth Exchange program has been a significant part of the LaCroix family life. Ralph and Darlene LaCroix have hosted seven exchange students from five different countries, as well as numerous Rotary Essex tour students coming through Dallas while on their tour of the United States. Their experiences were so favorable that Darlene joined the Allen Rotary Club as its first woman member in 1987 and later served as the club's first woman president in 1996-97. In addition, Darlene has served on the Board of the District 5810 Rotary Youth Exchange Committee for over seven years and has represented the district at the 1996 International Rotary Youth Exchange meeting in Calgary, Alberta, Canada. Here's the Darlene LaCroix story:

Darlene LaCroix

"Having been married for over forty years and raising six children of our own, it was the last thing on my mind, as my own brood were leaving the nest, to open our home to even one student from overseas - let alone the group that I now call my own. But one day while leaving church, we ran into an old friend, Joe Tepera, who stopped and asked if we would be interested in hosting a boy from Australia - it was through the Rotary Youth Exchange program and he would live with us for four months. I told Joe he was out of his mind - I was just about to wave goodbye to the last of our children and had no intention of cluttering up the place with another child - let alone a foreigner!

Well, my husband said, "don't listen to her Joe; if you get desperate, just give us a call." Joe said, "Oh, no we're not desperate - in fact, you're the first people we've asked. We just thought you were the type that would enjoy this kind of thing." Well, I looked at my old friend - he was the father of nine children - and they all were still at home! I said "Sure, Joe - if you can do it, so can we". And that's how it all began.

Andrew Pfitzner from Mt. Barker, Australia was our first and he was, and is, a honey. We learned fast that, for us, the only way to have an exchange student in our home was to treat him like our own child - we're pretty strict in our household - you *have* to be with as many children as we had. Andrew seemed to thrive on that discipline. A few years after we hosted Andrew, we had the great fortune to meet his charming parents. Since then, we have visited them twice in Australia, and they have been our guests here in the U.S. twice. Andrew's older brother, David, stayed with us for over a month while he was trekking 'round the world. And my daughter, Kris, attended Andrew's wedding in Mt. Barker. The entire family has become very dear to us.

While Andrew was in our home, our daughter, Kris, was chosen for the mini-exchange program to Germany, and thus we came to have two foreign exchange students in our home at the same time. It was so much fun - loveable, outrageous, out-going Andrew and a very shy, introvertish and cultured Vocker Bochen from Hannover, Germany. The three weeks we had with those two could fill a book. Let me say that Vocher became very close to us, even in this short amount of time. Now, almost ten years after the exchange, we still correspond with his family. They have visited us here, and we were fortunate to be able to visit them in Hannover. We were treated as visiting nobility and will always think of them in high regard.

Over the years, our house has expanded to accommodate a variety of personalities -- Uta Binder -- a wonderful Bavarian with whom we still correspond and hope that she will be getting married soon. She has been single too long.

And then there was Kim Russell...how fortunate we were to get Kim. Believe me, Norway's loss was our gain. She was a wonderful girl -- and while Kris was in Australia attending Andrews' wedding, she managed to stop in Brisbane on the way home for a great visit with Kim.

> ***Editor's Note:*** "It was almost 8:00 pm on Christmas eve, December 24, 1986. I received a phone call from someone who was unmistakably Australian. He identified himself as Peter Baker, Youth Exchange Officer of Rotary's District 960, in Brisbane, Australia. He called me from a list of International Youth Exchange officers (of which I was one) in District 581. It was Christmas Day in Brisbane (16 hours time difference). It seemed that he was desperate to make a placement for one of his "very best" exchange students. The student, Kim Russell, had been accepted by a Rotary district in Norway; however, Peter had just received notification that they could not accommodate her. And it was only three weeks before she was to depart! Could I possibly take her into the program? At that time, we had exchange arrangements with two other Australian districts...Sydney and Adelaide. We considered the Australian exchange students to be "the best in the system". I asked him to give me 24 hours...I would call him back the following day. My "ace in the hole" was Darlene LaCroix and the Allen Rotary Club. Fortunately,

> Darlene did not have a student that year, and the answer, immediately, was "Why not!" As an addendum to the story, four years later, Rose and I took the GSE team to Brisbane, Australia, and somehow Kim found out that we were coming and was in the greeting committee at the airport. Small world!"

Edwin Hofker from the Netherlands, Ricardo Gaellardo from Spain, and Annetta Roennigen from Norway round out our Rotary family. These students and all the students we have hosted through the Essex tour have added a dimension to our lives that can never be under-estimated.

The many times I have accompanied these kids to the airport to say goodbye as they leave to go home, I have had the feeling that these are the kinds of relationships that are so meaningful to world peace and harmony. Diplomats can sit around their shiny tables for months and not accomplish what these students accomplish every day all around the world.

I have talked to host parents from other exchange programs and, good as some of them are, acknowledging that I'm biased, I feel the screening process, the interviews (in which I have participated many times) the orientations, both here and abroad, plus the involvement of the counselors in the every day life of the exchange student (and I've been a counselor many times over), makes the difference in Rotary's program. We have dedicated people -- we know we have the best program in the world -- and we have thousands of former exchange students world wide who say that their experience abroad was the best thing that every happened to them in their young lives. Looking back, would we do it all over again?...**in a heartbeat!!**

I suppose that it's only natural for Rotary Youth Exchange officers to have favorites. In placing and knowing about 125 exchange students in the seven years between 1979-1986, I came to know many of them well and had lots of "favorites."

The district's first exchange student from Australia was a young lady from Sydney. As with all of the inbound students from Australia, Elisha Long had gone through a selection procedure where only about 10% of the applicants were chosen. She had been given a thorough indoctrination and came to our district with an excellent concept of what the International Youth Exchange program was all about.

I had placed her with the Hurricane Creek Rotary Club, in a rural area of our district. She came from a school with an enrollment of 4,000 and, while with one of her three host families, was enrolled in Gunter, Texas. High school enrollment: 200! During her indoctrination in Australia, she was told that the three most important things to remember about Youth Exchange were to "Adapt", "Adapt", and "Adapt" She did.

One of the myths about Youth Exchange is that the best placements are with Rotarians, or non-Rotarian families, with teenage children. Two out of the three of Elisha's host parents were *grandparents,* and the experience was great for each of them. One of the families was the Trumans, Corbie and Fran. Corbie is a member and past president of the Hurricane Creek,TX Rotary club. Here is the Truman story:

Corbie Truman (1924-1999)

In January of 1982 the Hurricane Creek Rotary Club welcomed their first foreign exchange student, Elisha Long, from Sydney, Australia. She brought great enthusiasm to this adventure in her life. While she was with us, she attended high school in Van Alstyne, Texas, where she concentrated on business subjects which would help her in the future.

Elisha was thrust into the culture of the three very small north centralTexas rural communities of Van Alstyne, Howe and Anna after living in the metropolitan area of Sydney. While this was a major frustration to her at first, she quickly adjusted to the new environment.

Elisha shared with us that she had five siblings and that she was the middle child. Both of her parents were practicing physicians, who over the years were stationed in Italy and the United States. Elisha was born in Philadelphia; she had dual citizenship in the U.S. and Australia. But she was quick to let you know that she was Australian. By the time she was twelve years of age, she had traveled around the world, living in the U.S. and Italy, and was fluent in Italian.

As part of her visit to this area, she was asked to speak and even present programs at various Rotary Clubs in the district. She was an instant hit. Her poise, intellect and very articulate manner of speaking, spiced with some Australian humor, endeared her to Rotarians everywhere she appeared.

Upon her return to Sydney in January, 1983, Elisha was accepted by the university for study in her chosen field, architecture. There she completed her bachelor and master degrees in conservational architecture. Before she started her graduate studies, she and two other graduate students traveled around the world, examining and sketching buildings in countries they visited. This trip took them to Singapore, India, northern Europe, to include Moscow and St. Petersburg in Russia, Italy and Spain. On her trip home she dropped by to see us. She showed us her sketches, which were to us wonderful pieces of art. She was most impressed by the magnificent designs left centuries ago by the Moorish builders in Spain.

A few years later Elisha visited us again on her way to England to be interviewed for a two year fellowship in conservational architecture. She was accepted and when she completed her study, she was hired by an architectural firm in York, England. She found time to get married to William Blackledge, a fellow architect in her firm. Then she was assigned to examine the outside of the dome of St. Paul's Cathedral in London. We visited London in June, 1995, met Elisha and Williams at St. Paul's, where they gave us a tour of the building. When we asked her why she went swinging around the outside of the dome, she said "Where else could I have London at my feet?" The couple is now back in Australia, awaiting their first child in June, 1999.

Often there are opportunities that change, not only the people directly involved, but people and organizations for years to come. The youth mini-exchange program is one of those opportunities. In 1977 our District 581 received an invitation to send a group of high school students to northern Japan for three weeks in return for the same opportunity for the Japanese young people to visit the U.S. While in the U.S., the Japanese would divide their time between our district, a district in California and a week in Evanston at Rotary International. **Dr. Ben Thomas,** past president of the Irving, Texas Rotary Club was asked to accompany the group on their trip to Japan.

When Dr. Ben talked about the trip he frequently said, "Off we went, under-trained, over-packed and pretty naive. We went through the usual stages of wondering whether or not we had brought some of the right students, but we discovered that through teamwork, everyone took a part and we just shared the responsibilities. It was great to see how the students grew in their experiences. In a very few days, the homesickness, acrophobia, claustrophobia, picky-eating were all drained out of our systems.

The experiences left long-lasting memories. We discovered eastern toilets were at floor level, we ate squid popsicles and we took every photo-op that same along. We also discovered the overwhelming hospitality of the Japanese people. Half of our time was spent in hotels and half in home stays, which put each student on his own a great deal of the time to interact and communicate with Japanese students their own age."

The initial mini-exchange program led our district to establish other short-term exchanges with Ireland, Germany and Italy. Dr. Thomas continued to devote a great deal of his time to Rotary through his tour of duty as District Youth Exchange Officer. The spirit of mini-exchange has helped many students re-think their values and even change their career choices. Crossing international borders is like going into a time warp.

Dr. Thomas says he still hears from some of the students from the 1977 exchange. One student is now a dentist and a Rotarian. Twenty-two years later, **Dr. Hank Jacobs** had a lot to say about his experience. "The Rotary Exchange Program to Japan in 1977 was a truly special experience.

Prior to that program, I had traveled a little. That trip took me to the other side of the world. We had challenges of language, culture and food. What we found were students just like ourselves who were eager to learn about our schools, our world and us. I learned that if you try, you can get to know someone and become friends in a short period of time and across many thousand of miles. This insight alone provided me with a useful tool for my life experiences. If I try to become a friend first, problems, if they do arise are more easily smoothed out."

Dr. Jacobs wishes that everyone could have an experience like his. He firmly believes that if everyone did, this world would be a much better place for us to live. He said that because of this experience, he wanted to become a Rotarian. Dr. Jacobs is now past president of the Irving Rotary Club and a multiple Paul Harris Fellow. The experiences just never end. They are passed on from one generation to the next!

Pete Herrmann, Dist. 5830

Pete Herrmann joined the Rotary Club of Gilmer, Texas, in 1977, and served as its president in 1986-87. From 1987-1995, he served the district as International Youth Exchange chairman, and was instrumental in establishing an "Outbound Camp" for exchange students from nine districts in Texas.

It all began in the most unlikely of places. In the back room of Cowboy's Country Cafe in Gilmer, Texas, in the middle of a defensive driving course, Rotarian Pete Herrmann and Lora Robinson began conversing. The subject: Rotary's International Youth Exchange program. Pete asked Lora about her son, Todd, and the possibility of his participation in the program. It was the beginning of a long, life-altering relationship.

In 1998, the Robinson family began by hosting a French exchange student during Rotary's Summer Exchange. It seemed to work out well and Todd was soon off to West Germany for a year-long stay and the experience of a lifetime. It was shortly before the beginning of the quiet revolution, which was to be the undoing of five decades of the Cold War. Rotary Youth Exchange provided much more than an unforgettable year with two German host families. It was a year of witnessing historic events, first-hand, up-close and very personal. Aside from achieving complete fluency in another language, the perspectives Todd gained from spending a year overseas were well worth delaying a year of college. In fact, Todd got quite a leg up in his collegiate studies. Upon returning to enroll at Baylor University in 1990, Todd "tested out" of 27 semester hours of German and 9 hours of business courses.

What an exciting year it was! But the friendships and host family relationships did not end after a year. For Todd, it was merely the beginning of a decade of travel, study, and employment, all of which can be traced back to his involvement with Rotary Youth Exchange.

Over the next three years, the Robinson family hosted eleven exchange students from six countries. Todd began his studies in International Business and German at Baylor, and spent every summer with Rotary host families in Europe, traveling, working and improving his language skills. In 1992, it all paid off. After unsuccessfully applying the previous year, Todd applied for and received one of the District 5830 Rotary International Ambassadorial Scholarships. Even after the prestigious scholarship had been awarded, a great deal of work remained for Todd. He was responsible for applying and gaining entry to one of three universities of his choice. He was responsible for clearing all course work and obstacles with the faculty at Baylor and the other universities. And finally, he was responsible for making all the necessary travel, living and diplomatic arrangements necessary to study abroad.

After three months of long-distance calling, meeting with professors, and dealing with coordinating over a seven-hour time difference, all of the criteria had apparently been met for Todd to attend the most prestigious business school in the German-speaking world...The St. Gallen School of International Economics, in St. Gallen, Switzerland. Only one detail stood in the way. Todd had not yet completed his undergraduate work at Baylor, which was required in Switzerland for American students to obtain a study visa. It seemed as though he might be forced to delay his plans yet another year, so he could obtain the necessary BBA degree. In a last-ditch effort, Todd called the headmaster's office in Gallen to plead his case, and to see if there was any possible exception to the rule.

Todd began his introduction in his best German, trying to make a good impression. To his utter surprise, he only got as far as...."I am a Rotary International Ambassadorial Scholar..." After that, the only reply he received was "No problem!" Need a visa, No problem! Need an apartment, No problem! Need prerequisite qualification to take graduate level courses? No problem, take whatever courses you'd like. Doctoral seminars, graduate level seminars, undergraduate linguistics, you're with Rotary, it's NO PROBLEM!

Right then and there, Todd realized what a powerful influence Rotary International has in this world. He later discovered the headmaster was a Rotarian, as was the Canton (state) Governor, and the head of the Swiss Federal Department of Education.

In the end, Todd finished 51 semester hours in 12 months, and earned a European Master's Degree, which was awarded to him the day he received his BBA at Baylor. The contacts he made during that year later provided the foundation he needed to gain employment at the United States International Trade Commission.

That led to his entrance into the American Graduate School of International Management (Thunderbird) at Glendale, Arizona, where Todd graduated in 1996 with his second Master's Degree in International Management. Finally, Todd was offered a position with Mercedes-Benz, and was moved to Stuttgart, Germany, as the global accessories manager for Mercedes- Benz passenger cars.. After several years, Todd had the opportunity to come home with a new venture, where he is currently the VP of Marketing and Sales at MI Technologies, Inc., in Gilmer, Texas.

This story began in 1989, when Todd became a foreign exchange student on the Rotary program. As you see, it progressed to a point, in 1992, when Todd had the opportunity to become a Rotary Ambassadorial Scholar. The third step in his Rotary experience was his induction into the Rotary Club of Gilmer this past year. He is now serving on the District 5830 Youth Exchange Committee. A decade has passed and he has come "full circle." What an exciting Rotary story!

Patrick L. O'Brien, Irving (TX) Rotary Club

In the late 1970's, I was attending my weekly Rotary Club meeting in Irving. The program that day was Youth Mini-Exchange. Our district was starting a youth mini-exchange with Japan. Dr. Ben Thomas, a past president of our club, presented the program and spoke of his experiences as the Rotary "chaperone" on his trip with 10 students to Japan the previous summer. I was spellbound about his experiences and the excellent opportunity it provided for the children of Rotarians.

During the next several years, we had many Youth Exchange programs at the club, when students who had been on summer exchanges came to the club and expressed their appreciation for the opportunity for having been a part of that exciting program. They talked about living with the families in a foreign country, and though the visit was for a short time, they felt as if they were part of the family.

In 1993, my older daughter, Kristi, had her opportunity to travel to Germany. Like most parents, I was nervous about sending my little girl to a far off place. But knowing of the experiences and background of the program, I knew that she would be well cared for.

Three weeks later, Kristi returned, literally a changed and grown person. The student who returned with my daughter was Susie, a very shy young East German. She was seeing the Free World for the very first time. Although her time with us was short, we believe we showed her a great deal about life in Texas.

Because of the experience my family had with Youth Exchange, I decided to volunteer in developing our district Mini-Exchange program the following year. I had volunteered to do a number of things in my own club, but it wasn't until I got involved with Youth Exchange that I really discovered what Rotary was all about. It meant meeting new Rotarians with different backgrounds, different careers, all working together in a most exciting program of Rotary. We all spend many hours planning each year's exchange. What are the rewards?.....it's simple. At the end of all of our exchanges, there is a family outing. Every participant, year after year, comes up to me and personally thanks me for sharing Rotary's Mini-Exchange with them.

Dr. Charles McAdams is a Professor in the Fine Arts Division of Brookhaven College, one of Dallas' seven community colleges. He is a past president of the Prestonwood (Dallas) Rotary Club and is currently a member of the Rotary Club of Carrollton-Farmers Branch.

Dr. Charles D. McAdams

During 1982, while in Norway with my family, we met a Norwegian family with a fifteen-year-old daughter. We visited in their home, shared a meal and fell in love with the culture. At that time, my wife, Sue, and I indicated to the family that many families sent their children to the U.S. for a year of schooling. We said that if they might be interested in sending their daughter, Siw-Jorunn, to Dallas, we would be happy to host her in our home. Over the next several months, international phone calls followed. Finally, an agreement was made to allow Siw-Jorunn to live with us for a year. The only thing left to do was get her a student visa.

Student visas are hard to come by and require either the I-20 application signed by a school district or a J-1 application from some sponsoring organization. The local school district had no interest in helping. We talked to other schools and intermediary organizations and learned that this was going to be very difficult. During one of our discussions, someone said that Rotary International had a youth exchange program. I was given the name of someone who referred me to someone else who referred me to Milton Kessel, Youth Exchange Officer for District 581.

After my initial phone call to Milton, we agreed to meet over lunch at Brookhaven Country Club to discuss the Rotary program. We met and Milton laid it all out very clearly. There were no direct, family to family, exchanges. Rotary operated district to district. In order for Siw-Jorunn to go anywhere, she needed to apply to her Rotary District and be accepted as a part of their program. She did that and then her Youth Exchange Officer contacted Milton, as the Rotary district officer in this area, and it was agreed that she would be able to come to the Dallas area. Next, Milton located a Rotary Club that would sponsor her, pay a monthly stipend and provide her with a counselor. The sponsoring club was the Dallas North Rotary Club; though it is normal in the Rotary program for a student to have more than one host family during her year's stay, it was agreed that we would be the host family for the entire year.

We made great preparations for her coming, none the least of which was the preparation of our twelve-year-old son, Trey. He was going to have a sister and he was going to have the opportunity to show her his country and teach her about how he did things in the U.S.

One hot August afternoon at D/FW airport, we waited with great anticipation for the plane to arrive. When Siw-Jorunn stepped off the plane. we saw, with horror, that she was dressed in heavy sweaters for winter. She asked, "Where are the mountains?" We collected her luggage, changed her into suitable clothing and took her home so that she could call her parents and tell them that she had arrived.

For dinner we took her to our favorite Mexican restaurant, El Fenix. As she spoke halting English, we assumed that she understood everything that we said to her. It was soon to become clear that she was eager to please, so she said "yes" to everything. We explained about tacos, enchiladas, tortillas and salsa. We ordered -- she ordered. We dipped the steamed tortillas into the salsa -- she dipped the steamed tortilla into the salsa. It was not until the smoke started coming out of her ears and the tears streamed down her cheeks that we realized she was just following our example. Her insides were on fire!. It took a little while to calm her down and stop the pain but she went valiantly on, trying everything. As it turned out, El Fenix became her favorite restaurant.

She soon settled in and we introduced her to the daughter of a friend who was part of the youth program at our church. There was a very active youth choir and she was invited to join. She had never had singing experience before, but she jumped right in. The new young friend and the youth choir were to play great roles in establishing her comfort zones.

Our son, Trey, attended The Greenhill School and Siw-Jorunn was accepted as well. By being involved in the Rotary International program, her tuition of several thousand dollars was waived. She played soccer and sang in the choir. She loved it immediately, because her new young friends attended there also. Siw-Jorunn had an immediate circle of young girl friends....boys would come later.

Siw-Jorunn's mother, Kari, was a registered nurse and that was what Siw-Jorunn wanted to be. In order to attain that goal, she would need to take chemistry. Problems began almost immediately. Siw-Jorunn was not used to the rigors of private school, and she quickly fell behind in her studies. She also got discouraged. We arranged for a tutor, who was only available during her soccer practice time. We determined that nursing was to come first and soccer second. Siw-Jorunn was not happy with the decision, but her parents had told her that we would make the decisions. She *did* pass chemistry....barely!

The Rotary District provided many youth exchange opportunities. There were week-end retreats, orientation sessions, trips together and many slumber parties. That year, the Rotary District Conference was held in Guadalajara, Mexico, and arrangements were made for all of the exchange students to go. The "manana" attitude was new to Siw-Jorunn but she loved the experience.

As a family, we had Tranksgiving in northwest Arkansas, a winter trip to Albuquerque, New Mexico, Christmas in Memphis, Tennessee, and spring break in New Orleans, Louisiana. We took her everywhere. Trey was anxious to show his sister everything.

While Siv-Jurann was with us, her parents came to visit, bringing their 14-year-old son, Ostein. Ostein spoke no English but he and Trey had a great time. The two families sharing a daughter went together to San Antonio for a weekend. We looked at the bluebonnets, swam at New Braunfels and ate on the River Walk in San Antonio. Siw-Jorunn was quick to tell her mother to watch out for the salsa and chili peppers. They also took her to San Francisco for a few days. The Youth choir at the church even went to New York City. We totaled up the miles she had traveled since leaving Norway, and it was over 25,000!

To date, each member of our family has been in Siw-Jorunn's home in Oslo. Her parents, brother, uncle, husband, mother-in-law and child have all been in our Dallas home.

The day Siw-Jorunn left Dallas was a sad one for our family. We were losing a daughter. Before going to the airport, we went to El Fenix for one last Mexican dinner!

Upon returning to Norway, Siw-Jorunn set about realizing her personal goal of becoming a nurse. It was interesting that one day, Helge, Siw-Jorunn's father, called to tell me that because of her having taken chemistry while at Greenhill, she was now "setting the curve" in her chemistry class. We had a good laugh talking about how long range goals can be achieved, even at the cost of short range plans. Siw-Jorunn is now a Registered Nurse. This Youth Exchange program has done exactly what it was intended to do: promote world peace and understanding, one person at a time. Because of the Rotary Youth Exchange program, we have also hosted a student from Cali, Colombia. This outstanding young man is now a graduate of Harvard University. His family also has visited in our home.

Because of our involvement with Youth Exchange, I became a Rotarian, with sixteen years of perfect attendance, am a past president, past Youth Exchange Officer, former Alternate Responsible Officer of the United States Information Service, past District Chair of International Service, Paul Harris Fellow and Benefactor. I have "made-up" meetings in Seattle, New York, Mexico, England and Russia.

As Youth Exchange Officer, I have had the experience of going to the airport to see American students leave and foreign students arrive. I've been involved with the outbound program, the inbound program, the mini-exchange, many trips to Rotary dinners and events and the memorable orientation trips to The Country House, with its own secluded cemetery. The Country House is another story just by itself. It has been most rewarding to see new students grow and be willing to share some of their experiences and that growth with others. Youth Exchange Works!

11

ENJOY ROTARY

Clifton Rogers

One of the most "recognizable" Rotarians in Distrist 5810 is Clifton Rogers, a member and past president of he Rotary Club of Oak Cliff (Dallas) Texas. "Cliff" is pulpit minister of the Edgefield Church of Chirst in Dallas. Since his profession has created changes in the location of his ministry, he has been a member of several Rotary Clubs, including the Brazesport, Texas Rotary Club, of which he served as president. He has presented programs on the Rotary Foundation, or on his favorite subject, "Enjoy Rotary", to virtually every club in the District. In addition, he has been "the" Rotary Foundation source of information for many years. During Rotary Foundation Month (November each year), he prepares and distributes an up-to-date publication (3,500 copies) to the 58 clubs telling about our district's participation in the programs of the Foundation. Cliff sez:

ENJOYING ROTARY!

Here's hoping you enjoy being a Rotarian. I do -- not with the bubbling enthusiasm of a newly inducted member (Gilmer, Texas, 1942), but with the firm and continuing joys of fellowship and service -- past, present and anticipated future. Your contemplation of "Do I enjoy Rotary?" will be personalized as you remember your experiences and joys through the years of your fellowship -- even as I review some of mine.

"Now I'm A Rotarian"...Wonderful!...What a thrilling time this was. Excitement, joy, expectation. I didn't really understand what the person proposing me for membership meant when he expressed the anticipation that I would *become* a Rotarian. I had already been inducted, given a pin and a badge. Of course, I came to know what he meant. What a bank of satisfaction and memories---fellowship, service, making a difference! Think of your being a Rotarian. You are in a Rotary Club, where everybody is somebody, and where friendship and fun, service and satisfaction constitute a rewarding way of life. Common factors are: attendance (including make-ups), involvement, friendship, joy, optimism. Obviously these are linked with vision, expectation, responsibility, dependability, appreciation.

"We are a service club." Projects and plans in community service, vocational service, and international service are vibrant parts of a thriving, happy Rotary Club. Involvement of members is part of the success and joy of any project. "Partial success" need not be a downer. There has been effort and dedication.

Rotary has been, and is, an especially joyful part of my life. I have maintained 48 years of perfect attendance, which attests to the fact that I enjoy the fellowship of the weekly meetings. Rotary has not taken the place of family, of employment, of church. It has its own special place. When our sons were small boys, they thought one name of a brand of cigar was "El Rotarian." (No, I'm not a smoker.) And to be a Paul Harris fellow is ever so meaningful to me, as is the knowledge that my wife also is, as are our son, daughter-in-law, granddaughter and grandson. The cynic may think, "Three years after the $1,000.00 has been given, that full amount is committed to some good work, and THAT'S IT." No, no, that's just the beginning...looking far into the future in which many, many lives know the difference.

How wonderful long-term friendships in Rotary are, and how tender are memories of friendships that were. In your imagination, sit with me in a funeral chapel where the sons of one of our Rotary Club's past presidents are memorializing their dad. One says, concerning Dr. William L. Hall, "Dad would use a very small brush and some red fingernail polish to put a little red "H" on items that belonged to him. In fact, he would put a little red "H" on items he thought belonged to him. Sometimes, he would put a little red "H" on items he thought *should* belong to him." Ah, we're quietly chuckling. Now the son points at us with the sweep of a hand,

"Whether or not you know it, there is a little red "H" on the heart of each of you...Dad claimed you." Now that lump in each of our throats becomes very hard to swallow.

Indeed, Rotary goes on enthusiastically and joyfully, whether or not you know it. Believe me!

Rotary Friendship Exchange

PDG Tyler Baker, Dist. 5890

Tyler Baker has been a member of Rotary since 1976, and served as president of the Brazosport (TX) Rotary Club in 1986-1987. He served as District Governor 1990-91. Since that time, he was Group Study Exchange team leader to Brazil in 1994 and Norway in 1997.

Rotary Friendship Exchange is Rotary's exchange program for Rotarians and their families. Friendship Exchanges allow Rotarians the opportunity to experience another culture first-hand in the homes of Rotarians in other countries. The exchanges are reciprocal, and last anywhere from a few days to more extended visits. Participating in a Friendship Exchange offers Rotarians an opportunity to make a personal contribution to advancing world understanding while expanding their own horizons. Since the programs inception, thousands of Rotarians have availed themselves of this unique cultural opportunity and many long-standing friendships have resulted.

There are two types of Friendship Exchanges. The first is a club-to-club visitor program in which individual Rotarians, who may be accompanied by a family member, spend a few days in the home of a Rotarian in another country. It is expected that guests who participate in this type of exchange will reciprocate by serving as hosts for later exchanges.

The second type of exchange is a district-to-district team program in which four to six Rotary couples visit several communities in a host district for a period of up to a month. The number of couples and/or length of stay may be varied by agreement of the districts involved. The following year, the guest district hosts a team from the host district. The team program is the ultimate personalized group tour.

My own experience started in 1979 when District Governor Jim Carrell made his official visit to the Brazesport Rotary Club. In his explanation of the many facets of Rotary, he mentioned there was to be a meeting in Houston for those interested in a Friendship Exchange with District 1060 in England. I brought this information home and discussed the possibilities with Mildred. We have always enjoyed traveling. She didn't seem to be very interested in the thought of staying with someone whom we had never met. However, she and I attended the meeting and were among the 26 couples from District 5890 who made the journey to the Birmingham area of the Midlands in June, 1980. It was a 15-day visit with three hosts for five days each. The trip was most enjoyable to everyone. We had the opportunity to see the area from the view of the hosts, not as a tourist. It was great to visit in the homes of Rotarians, share family experiences and become friends in a way that would be impossible without the exchange program of Rotary. The only down side is that it spoils you for conventional travel and you realize how much you are missing by not visiting with your Rotary friends in the Rotary World.

The exchange of June, 1980 has created a better understanding between the participants of both districts. There is, after 19 years, a continuing relationship between the Rotarians of both countries with phone calls and home visits occurring on a continuing basis.

In 1984 we established a Club-to-Club Friendship Exchange with District 417 in Mexico City. A Rotarian from our club was making up at Tlainepantlia and suggested a visit from their club to ours. It has been a successful relationship since its inception.

In 1985 we had our first visit with District 5360 in Canada. There were 26 couples who enjoyed the culture north of the border. Rotarians in Edmonton and Calgary hosted us for four days each. The group flew from Houston to Edmonton and then took a bus from there to Calgary after the visit. District 5360 arranged for the exchange to take place during the

Calgary Stampede. We also visited Lake Louise and Banff during that trip. The following year the Canadians journeyed to Texas and were hosted by D/5890. Since that time, there have been other exchanges between these districts.

In 1992, as a spin-off from the GSE program during 1991, we were invited to District 2690 in the Okayama City area of Japan. It was a great learning experience to visit Japan, live in their homes, experience a new diet, and to be hosted in the most courteous manner possible. We visited auto manufacturing plants, biomedical facilities, and many cultural locations. We later hosted the Japanese in our district. Many relationships continue.

Rotary Friendship Exchange is funded entirely by the individuals who participate. Generally, guests are responsible for their travel expenses and personal spending (souvenirs, etc.) Host are expected to provide housing, meals and sight-seeing -- the same courtesies that would be extended to a visiting friend.

It has been our experience that it is best for the exchange chairmen of the two districts to work a schedule that has a different host after four or five days. The number of couples and/or length of stay may be varied by agreement of the districts involved, based on distance traveled and number of hosts available.

In summary, after 19 years of experience with the Rotary Friendship Exchange, I have found that it provides an outstanding opportunity to extend your circle of Rotary friends. We have friends in Mexico, Canada, Great Britain and Japan that we could not have met without the Friendship Exchange program. It is a learning experience that is not available in any other format in the world. You make friends that last a lifetime. Your horizon is extended to encompass the whole Rotary World. I would recommend that each Rotarian, Club and District become involved with this great program.

Recreational Fellowships

They're some of the best kept secrets of all of the Rotary programs, yet there are over 20,000 Rotarians throughout the world who take part in the "fun and games" of the organization....the 40 different groups of Rotary's recreational fellowship programs. They include stamp collectors, amateur-radio enthusiast, chess players, skiers and many, many others.

One of the most active in participation is the International Fellowship of Flying Rotarians, known as the IFFR. Started in 1965 it now boasts a membership of 1,650 world-wide Rotarians who "just love to fly!" Each year in June, a good many fly in to the International Convention in private planes.

PDG Vactor Stanford, 45-year member of the Rotary Club of Fair Park (Dallas) TX, became a modern-day Charles Lindbergh, when he and four other IFFR members decided to form an entourage of their own private planes from the USA to Birmingham, England, to attend the 1984 Rotary International Convention. Vac was president of IFFR at the time. They met up in Boston, where they began their historic journey. Here's the story:

PDG Vactor (Vac) Stanford

Although I have had many memorable flights while accumulating over 5,000 hours of pilot in command time, I believe the flight to the 1984 Rotary International Convention in Birmingham, England would have to be my choice of most memorable. I had flown my wife and children to many of the Rotary Conventions in the USA, but they were not interested in flying across the Atlantic in a private plane! So I enlisted a couple of other Rotarians to go with me in my plane, which was a twin engine Piper Navajo with 350 horse engines and a cruising speed of over 200 nautical MPH. Our flight began in Dallas with five in the plane, three being pilots and the other two were wives of the other two Rotarians.

Before leaving, we had an extra 300-gallon aviation gasoline tank installed in the cabin immediately behind the co-pilot's seat and connected so that it could be pumped into the mains, when needed.

We flew to Boston, where we spent the first night having dinner with friends. The next day we flew to Moncton, New Brunswick, where we had agreed to meet with the four other planes that were to accompany us on the trip. It turned out that ours was the only plane there, the others having taken different routes from different parts of the U.S. This didn't concern us too much, since we had agreed that before any of us left to cross the Atlantic we would meet at Frobisher Bay, Nova Scotia.

The next stop was at a city about halfway to Frobisher, where we gassed up and took of for Frobisher in weather that was getting worse all the time. Since we were on a flight plan and had de-icing equipment, it didn't bother us too much, although we worried about the other planes that were not as well equipped as we were. But they all made it.

We took off the next morning with a ceiling of about 500 feet. About an hour out, planning our flight to Sondrestrom, Greenland, the clouds broke for a few minutes so that we could see land below us. We discovered that the bays on the west side of Davis Straits were turned so that we figured we were heading about 90 degrees north of our intended route. We also figured out that we shouldn't have been relying on magnetic headings, but rather should have been flying true headings, because the longitudinal lines that close to the North Pole were so close together. So we took a 90 degree turn to the right and agreed that if we didn't pick up a radio or radar signal within 30 minutes, we would return to Frobisher and start over. About twenty minutes later we received a call from the U.S.radar outpost at Tule, Greenland (on the dewline) asking if we were N666HC...we admitted that we were, and they asked "Where are you guys going, to Russia?" They told us that we were 90 miles North of our planned route, but it didn't matter since we were the only plane out there and we were now headed in the right direction!

In about an hour the Sondrestrom radar picked us up and we made a GCA instrument approach into their landing strip. We spent one night there and the next morning found that it had snowed during the night, so we cleaned our wings off and departed for Reykavik, Iceland (735 nautical miles). A very enjoyable flight, and we spent two exciting days in Iceland being squired by Rotarians who a few years earlier had been GSE team members to Dallas. Our next stop was Stornaway, Scotland where we refueled to take off for Glasgow. Next stop....Birmingham and the International Convention.

After the convention, we flew to Dusseldorf, Germany to meet with another group of GSE team members who had visited us in Dallas. Then back to Stornaway to check out of Europe and home by the same route we had covered flying over. It was, indeed, a most memorable trip!

I, along with other local IFFR members, have flown nine GSE teams to visit NASA in Houston. In 1984, two of us flew the inbound GSE team from Germany to Guadalajara, Mexico, where our annual district conference was being held.

All over the world, members of IFFR have provided "opportunities for service"...and have had fun doing it!

Charles D. McAdams, Jr.

We should enjoy what we do, right? Well, then does it not follow that we should enjoy our memberships in organizations? Enjoy Rotary! How many of us really do that? I think that the answer is, "Not enough"; otherwise so many Rotarians would not be dropping by the wayside. Let's look at the many ways in which our Rotary membership might be enjoyed or maybe enjoyed more, so that we would want to share our satisfaction with others.

Because a person is inducted into membership in Rotary, does that make a person a Rotarian? Maybe being a Rotarian means becoming aware of the many facets of what many of us feel is a jewel of an organization. Some feel like they belong as soon as they are presented as club members, just because they have heard so much about the organization. They feel good when they get their Rotary pin. Others grow into this business of "being" a Rotarian only after being at a club meeting or at other club meetings as they "make-up." Some gain that feeling only after an involvement in a project or an activity. Still others gain that feeling through the many friendships encouraged by common interests. There are many that experience feelings of elation, optimism and joy that come from seeing just what their club, their district or the international organization can do.

Each year the opportunities for service increase because of the changes in leadership within the over 500 Rotary Districts, and the President of Rotary International, as well. This comes about through their implementation of new programs and services. The beginning of the Rotary year is a perfect time for all Rotarians to stop, take stock, and set new goals, objectives and activities. Different people have different ideas and there is always plenty of room for opportunities. These opportunities are, as you know, channeled into the Four Avenues of Service: Club Service, Vocational Service, Community Service and International Service. These are spelled out by the new administrations as they make their plans for the new Rotary year. This is always a good time to stop and say, "Thank You" to those who have given of themselves. A pat on the back for a job well done is always a positive stroke. Add a good pep talk to the mix from someone who has been around the block enough times to recognize what a little encouragement can do, and you can really enjoy your Rotary experiences. You see, sometimes we never really know when we have touched somebody. We sometimes know that when they begin to model their type of behavior that encourages "Service Above Self." That feels <u>good.</u>

Regular involvement is a must for any organization that hopes to sustain itself. It is critical to be there if you, as an individual, want to make it worthwhile. You are important as a role model and as a supporter. You can't be counted if you are not there to stand up for what you believe. You cannot help shape the future if you are not there, and you can't possibly enjoy what you don't participate in. You have to be there to share your experiences and encourage others by saying things like, "Let me tell you how much fun we had when we......"

Club programming is important to this enjoyment. When was the last time you told a non-Rotarian friend how much you enjoyed listening to so-and-so present your Rotary Club program. You can help develop those programs when you share information from other programs. "Lets get ....over to speak to us."

Have you ever presented a program? One of the best ways to learn about something is to be put on the spot to talk about it. This should be a requirement of every club. Introduce yourself to your own club by giving them your own thoughts about your vocation or avocation. It is a great icebreaker. It also serves to help you understand what it takes to present a good program. If you put them to sleep, they will only remember you as their best anesthesiologist.

One of the great opportunities for enjoyment of Rotary is to attend other club meetings. Everyone needs "make-ups." Get to know other clubs. Make friends while you're there. Every club has its own personality. You can get a lot out of Rotary by learning how others accomplish worthwhile projects. Others have fun, too. Try to find out how. Social events are great ways to enjoy Rotary and there are far too many opportunities to even make a list. Look for them....and you'll find them.

We are, after all, a *service* organization. This is what we are about. Let's get about it! Good leadership requires good followship. Everyone, no matter how busy they are, can do something. Don't hide behind a weak excuse. Hide behind a good idea or a good project. It is amazing how much a person can learn from an experience....even a bad one! Not everyone can design a house; some need to hammer the nails. Be sure to be sincere in your thanks for being included in the experience. Thank the people who planned it and, above all, thank those who worked by your side. It make things a lot more enjoyable to be around someone who encourages others, than it is to be around someone who always finds reasons why things did not work out well.

Do you have friends? Of course you do. Have you asked them to join Rotary? Rotary needs to grow and you are the one who can make it happen.....one person at a time. Have fun with your friends and make it happen in Rotary. You have to invest in order to reap benefits. Invest in Rotary by making deposits in membership and the club will reap the benefits of having more ideas and more hands. This means progress.....and you are the key!

12
COMMUNITY SERVICE

The structure of most Rotary Clubs in the world is divided into four "avenues of service." One of these four is designated as "Community Service" and it is anticipated that all clubs will seek out and recognize the needs that exist within their community...to provide whatever service, both physically and financially, that they can.

It is also one of the duties of a district governor to visit every club in his/her district at least once, to provide counsel and assistance in the operation of their club.

While I was Governor, on one of these visits to a club in an affluent area of our district, I asked the club president what type of fund raising event they had each year. The president said, "none." I then asked, "How do you come up with club funds to support your various charities?" The answer was, "There really isn't a need in this up-scale community, so we don't have to raise any money." I mentioned that within a five-mile radius of his club's location there existed plenty of "opportunities for service."

There were 40 clubs in Dallas County at that time. Within a short distance of the club I visited was another club in an even more affluent area. That club: The Rotary Club of Addison, Texas. Here is an interesting story of how they found, and started providing a wonderful service to their community. The project is now in its tenth year. It is told by their current president, Frederic Silver, and past president Bill Wallace. They have both been involved in the project from its inception.

Frederic Silver and Bill Wallace

"It was certainly not by accident but by design that the Addison Rotary Club was able to establish and develop what many consider to be *the* outstanding community service project in our Rotary district. It started in 1989 with a club outing -- an enjoyable golf tournament. As well as a great club activity, the tournament was a financial success.

With some additional funds in our treasury, we sought out a number of charities in our area which might benefit from our support. One of our members was familiar with an organization called "Bryan's House," a home that offered loving care for children and families affected by HIV/AIDS. Its mission: to respond to the needs of these families by providing cost-free, medically-managed child care and family support service. All of our club members agreed that Bryan's House would be a most worthy beneficiary of funds generated from the tournament.

In 1990, we developed a 5-year plan to make the Bryan's House tournament one of the key Dallas fund-raising events. We contacted one of the major network TV stations, WFAA Channel 8, for its support...and received it. This resulted in their leading sportscaster, Brian Jensen, becoming our tournament spokesperson. The tournament was named, "The Brian Jensen's Bryan's House Open." Brian has remained with the tournament these past nine years.

To prepare for the first tournament, all of our members were fully informed about the plans and every member was asked to commit a total personal effort to insure the success of the project. Since that time, each member does something to "service" the tournament, whether it be raising money through solicitation of sponsorships or volunteering to work at the golf course on the day of the tournament. Even prospective members are told about the tournament and are well-informed of the importance of the event.

Little did we realize in 1990 that from the original $25,000 grant, 10 years later, the Addison Rotary Club will have given over $1,500,000 to Bryan's House!

As we reflect on the past, while preparing for the 10th Annual Bryan's House Open, we know that the Addison Rotary Club has played a significant role in the success of Bryan's House, providing it the needed impetus at an early state of its development, gaining for it much needed funds and community recognition of a service being well provided to a community where no other organization or facility existed."

The following article, written by Mr. Huntley Paton, publisher of the Dallas Business Journal and reprinted with his permission, reflects the marvelous image of Bryan's House and reinforces the decision some 10 years ago by the Addison Rotary Club to provide financial and personal support to this most worthy organization.

A kind place, a cruel disease

"They like the same toys. That's what struck me as I was peering at the infants and toddlers in the nursery at Bryan's House.

They like the same toys as my son. One little girl pounded on the big, yellow "play" button of a music box identical to one my wife and I bought for our son a while back. A little boy rolled around on a coloful play mat exacly like the one at my house.

Kids are the same everywhere, of course, especially at play. The difference is that my son, praise God, is healthy, while most of the kids at Bryan's House aren't. Seeing them play with the same goofy abandon as any normal child was a cheerful thing; seeing them surrounded by toys identical to my son's, though, got to me, because it forced me to imagine my son as the ill one.

Those few seconds of imagining were scary enough. For these kids and their families, it's real life all the time.

Bryan's House provides medical services, child care and family support services to local kids affected by the HIV/AIDS epidemic. It started with the capacity to serve nine kids and has grown dramatically, a model of love and caring as heart-warming as the epidemic is heart-breaking.

Cynthia Nunn, the executive director, said Bryan's House has to turn away 10 kids or more every day. Fortunately, Bryan's House is buying land and office space near St. Paul Medical Center, which will allow it to more than double its capacity. When the move occurs months from now, more kids who live under the cruelest of circumstances (roughly 94% of the kids served by Bryan's House live below the poverty line in addition to living with HIV) will benefit from the kindest of programs.

"This is a happy place," said Sherfyl Reid, development director at Bryan's House. That surprises a lot of people. But she is correct. It is a happy place. On our visit, a passel of older kids came back from a field trip, loud and happy. They buzzed and chatted and bounced around with that uncontrollable energy kids have and, moments later, all of them were on their nap palettes, snoozing. A good day.

The staff at Bryan's House pursues "good days" the way you and I chase profits. Every day. For many of the kids, good days are in short supply and can end fast. For a house filled with sick kids, Bryan's House has a powerfully healthy effect on visitors. It's a noble place and nobility is pretty damn rare in our society today. It's curious, but Reid smiles in a certain way that I don't recall seeing often in business circles. Maybe it's peace of purpose.

Bill Wallace, with the Ackley Financial Group and a member of the Addison Rotary Club, can pitch business with the best of them, but he is a different person inside Bryan's House. He's been devoting hours and hours to the cause for years. "When one of those kids crawled up into my lap, I knew I was in the right place."

Jane Henderson, MEd, LPC

Jane Henderson is *not* a Rotarian; however, her husband, Charlie Henderson, has been a member of the Rotary Club of Lancaster, Texas, since 1984 and served as its president in 1988. He is currently an Assistant Governor of District 5810 for the year 1999-2000. As a retired school teacher, Jane tells about her wonderful experiences in a second vocation...tutoring!

Tutoring: A Life Changing Experience

"It is not the threat of death, illness, hardship, or poverty that crushes the human spirit; it is the fear of being alone and unloved in the universe.".....Anthony Welsh.

Webster describes a tutor as a private teacher; to teach, instruct in small groups, especially individually. Some teachers, parents and/or children would describe a tutor as an angel of mercy. As a child in early elementary years, math was easy for me, but reading was the mysterious skill that my brain could not deal with successfully. No one knew that I was Dyslexic. I am not even sure the word existed back in the early 50's. I just knew that I felt stupid and the teachers did not seem to like me very much, either.

I am told that I was overjoyed when it came time to start school, and that my comments after the first day included, "if I had known that it was going to be like this, I never would have started this mess." And yet, I have been going to school for the last fifty years, as a student, teacher, consultant, or counselor. You see, there was that very special person who gave me the most valuable thing she had to give, her time. Between the third and fourth grades I had a reading tutor. She made me feel so smart and so special and so capable. She unlocked the doors of my mind and the skills that were hidden by Dyslexia. I will forever be grateful to that precious lady, Mrs. Ragsdale. Every child needs someone to believe in them.

My life was changed immeasureably by a tutor, and I fieel that I want other students to have the opportunity. I am confident that I have gained most from the experiences. It is wonderful to see children blossom, gain their self confidence and succeed in the learning experience. Research done by Arthur Stone at the State University of New York shows that positive events have a stronger positive impact on the immune system than negative ones; therefore strengthening the power of a person's body to fight off illnesses. Hawaiians call if *kokua,* which means to render assistance and relief to others.

Recently, I was told a story by my cousin that warmed my heart. She and her husband own multiple business in Beaumont where I grew up and taught school for several years. One morning they were waiting for the auditor to show up in the main office of Smart's Trucking. When the young lady arrived, she apologized for being late. She told them that she had to sell her grandmother's home, which she inherited upon her death. While the accountant was in the office, the young lady mentioned that she had been one of my math students in junior high school....that she had a terrible time with her fears and failures in mathematics. She told my cousin that the tutoring I did with her helped her overcome the fears which she had, and that she went on to graduate with a degree in mathematics and had become a CPA. What a joy for me to hear of her success!

I had mentioned earlier in this story about my having been Dyslexic. Only after we married, did I find out that my husband, Charlie, had the same malady, shared the same embarrassment as most dyslexic do until they *"have been turned around"*. He attributes his having attained two college degrees to being tutored successfully.

Don't miss the opportunity for a most heart-warming experience.... tutor a student in your local public school!

Making A Difference

Each year, the president of Rotary International develops a "theme" for the upcoming Rotary year to inspire Rotarians to serve their community, their country and the world. During the 1992-93 Rotary year, the theme announced by President Cliff Dochterman was "Real Happiness is Helping Others", which challenged Rotarians all over the world to use their talents and expertise to help improve the welfare of their own communities.

Through implementation of that theme, it was realized that Rotary Clubs, with concerted and focused effort on a project, could make a real difference to any needy individual or group.

But it does not take an organization or group to "make a difference." You, as an individual Rotarian, can.

At the beginning of the 1999 fall school term, I started tutoring sixth grade math at Preston Hollow grade school in North Dallas. I had thought about doing it last year...and finally said, "Why not?" I was there for one hour classes, twice a week. The class was the first of the day, so that I was through by 9:30 am. and could spend the rest of the day on other things I had planned.

To those of you who have not visited your neighborhood public school within the last few years...*you should!*

Here's what I found. Preston Hollow was built in the early 60's for grades 1 through 6 to accommodate 450 students. It now "houses" 890. Enrollment is approximately 50% Hispanic, 35% black, and 15% white, which is a typical mix in the Dallas Independent School District. A great percentage of the students are from one-parent families. About 50% of the sixth grade students were not at that school the previous year.

Rose and I have lived in the Preston Hollow school area for 51 years. Each of our four children went through that school. I was active in the Dad's Club and PTA. I feel as if I have an "investment" in the school, and in the simple expression, I wanted to give something back.

I was neither naive, nor was I totally surprised by the experience. Based on my evaluation of the educational level of these students compared to the years our children were in Preston Hollow, I would rate it no higher than 70%.

What is currently the #1 focus (or #2 behind Social Security) of our federal government in domestic issues? Public Education. There will be billions of dollars spent each year in an effort to improve the system. It will take more than money.

I gave myself a challenge at the beginning of the school year. My challenge was to bring my four students along during the year, so that each of them would pass the TAAS (Texas Assessment of Academic Skills) test. I was very pleased when I received a call from the 6th grade teacher a week before school was out for the year that all of them had passed!

My challenge to you is this....take two hours a week out of the 168. No matter what field of work you are in, whether you're retired, semi-retired, working full time, a young family man, whatever....Just Do It! You *will* make a difference.

Milton Kessel

13

ROTARY INTO THE 21ST CENTURY

Rotary International, now with almost 30,000 clubs and a million and a quarter (plus) members throughout he world, is governed by an international president and a board of directors of sixteen members, representing clubs in 164 countries.

The president of R.I. officially serves a one-year term. However, he must have served previously as a district governor, as well as an international director. In most cases, every R.I. president has put in many, many years of Rotary service prior to his having been selected as president, and becomes so involved and dedicated to his Rotary service, that he continues to serve long after his one-year term as president is over.

Such is the case with Dr. Cliff Dochterman, who served Rotary International as its president in 1992-1993. His Rotary theme for the year was, "Real Happiness is Helping Others", and that theme might well have been an appropriate title for this book. In 1995, he authored a publication called, "The ABCs of Rotary", which many, including this editor, consider to be the *premier* booklet of Rotary information for both new and old members of Rotary.

In 1998, International President Jim Lacy named a commission to make a study of "Rotary's Dream for the Future." He asked Cliff Dochterman to chair that very important committee. I feel that it is very appropriate to conclude this book with his comments from that study.

Past International President Cliff Dochterman (1992-1993)

President Jim Lacy asked the Rotary world to Dream For The Future and follow those Rotary Dreams...and that they did.

Some 2,000 dreams, and a few nightmares, came from every corner of the world to the Dreams For The Future committee. As I read and summarized the hundred of hand-written and computer-printed pages, bound documents, video tapes, and personal research papers, I recalled some words of Paul Harris in his book, My Road To Rotary. He said, "The spirit of Rotary should be the spirit of the Renaissance. We need men of microscopic vision who will explore the molecules, atoms, and electrons, but we also need men of telescopic vision who will explore the stars." What a prophetic statement.

Rotary certainly has a multitude of members with "microscopic vision." They examine every molecule and atom of our organization. They are concerned about attendance, classifications, financial statements, campaign violations, and the complexity of our worldwide organization. Rotarians with microscopic vision see these issues as vital for Rotary's future.

On the other hand there are many Rotarians with "telescopic vision," who look to the stars and beyond. These are the Rotarians who see Rotary International moving mountains, turning deserts into green acres, building a world without war; protecting the planet from asteroids and comets in the atmosphere; and eliminating the pain and suffering of every disease known to man. These visionaries are men and women who see no limits to the capacity of Rotary service in the world.

Rotary's future must certainly include dreams with both microscopic and telescopic vision. Where is Rotary going in the 21st century? What happens after our PolioPlus program? We expect to achieve our goal of a world without polio by the end of the year 2000. PolisPlus has given Rotary a new status in the world, as an organization which has the capacity to do huge things. The world is looking at Rotary with renewed respect and expectations. Many people, including large numbers of Rotarians, believe that Rotary has the capacity to do extremely significant things in the world.

So, the first recommendation for the future is a program labeled, "Rotary For A Healthy World." Rather than proposing Rotary International adopt a single disease for special emphasis after PolioPlus, it is recommended that Rotary Clubs worldwide develop active programs to control and treat diseases which especially afflict their communities, such as leprosy, tuberculosis, measles, dengue fever, malaria and other endemic diseases. Worldwide Rotary projects could enhance the lives of millions of people, and especially children, by preventing and controlling disease.

In response to overwhelming proposals from Rotary Clubs, another recommendation is a worldwide network for "Rapid Response to Disaster Relief." While Rotarians have been helpful and effective in the past, it is urged that Rotary develop a large scale disaster relief program. The technique used in many countries, called "emergency and aqua boxes" which provide supplies necessary for a single family prepared and stored for ready distribution, may offer a specific approach for Rotarians.

The issue of world hunger and poverty is the third proposal. The Committee recommends that Rotary launch an international collection and distribution system for food surpluses, preventing food waste, and working with governments and private carriers to transport food to the millions who live ion areas of acute hunger. Our primary effort must be to help people everywhere become self-sufficient so that they can either produce or purchase the food they need.

Health, hunger, poverty, and emergency relief are dependent upon one vital resource — clean water. We propose that Rotary Clubs make a commitment for "Clean Water For Every Community." To achieve clean water for every community, it is recommended that Rotary establish incentive-based Rotary Foundation grants to promote the construction of water wells, collection receptacles and tanks, filtration and purification systems, as well as water conservation and sanitation projects. We propose that

Rotary Clubs accept a goal of 10,000 water projects per year for a 10 year period to make an impact on the world.

The most prevalent of all the dreams, was to ensure that all children have opportunities for basic education, health, food and opportunities to grow to meaningful adulthood. A fifth major recommendation is to ensure that by 2025, all children of the world have access to primary education. This dream is particularly significant because we urge that special emphasis by given to the education for girls in all nations to enhance the quality and stability of the home, the birthright of babies and the resulting balance of world populations. The evidence is abundantly clear that education for girl children is the most effective means to meet critical problems of worldwide overpopulation.

In addition to education for youngsters, the recommendations urge Rotary to reach out to orphaned and abandoned children, to facilitate adoption processes and provide for their needs through Rotary sponsored projects. If Rotary is to address seriously the plight of children, the Committee proposes that Rotarians establish a special Children's Trust within the Permanent Fund of the Rotary Foundation to support future projects for children throughout the world.

In the coming decades, a renewed Rotary focus must be directed to the environment and alternative energy sources. In addition to expanded programs to Preserve Planet Earth, it is recommended that the R.I. Board challenge all clubs and districts to plant one million trees worldwide each year for ten years to enhance the environment and replace deforested areas. At the same time, Rotary International will ask clubs to explore alternative sources of energy, such as sun, hydrogen, biomass, wind and water energy sources, which are environmentally sustainable and will reduce the use of limited fossil fuels.

To achieve these noble objectives may require some basic changes in Rotary operations in the coming decades.

The first of these recommendations is to move Rotary International into a new level of telecommunications and technology. The Rotary of the future will adopt widespread uses of new technologies, such as teleconferencing, internet communications, Power-point presentations, satellite communications, automated translations and other electronic resources to enhance the effectiveness of club operations, conferences, training and service projects. These steps into new technology will make the organization much more attractive to younger members.

The Committee reviewed dozens of "dreams" for Rotary to come to grips with policies which may have fulfilled a need ninety years ago , but are not relevant to the current business and professional world of the year 2000. It is clear that the Rotary world must simplify many policies and types of memberships, providing some creative new options for memberships and classifications, including corporate, family associate and spouse memberships.

Another important step is to enhance the quality of Rotary Clubs, many of whom function under the name of Rotary, with little or no activities or service programs. It is desirable for Rotary to adapt a clear and consistent program within an umbrella of specific themes. The Committee felt strongly that Rotary's effectiveness is greatly diminished, rather than enhanced, by the constant change in annual themes and program emphases established by Rotary international Presidents and boards of directors. Rotary programs should be clearly understood with a consistent and understandable message, known to all Rotarians and the general public.

This brings up another vital topic — the public image of Rotary International in the world. The committee believes that the time is now for Rotary International and The Rotary Foundation to make a long term commitment to implement a professional program of high quality institutional information in the public media. We urge the Rotary leadership to step forward with a major effort to tell the public what Rotary is and Rotary does. Rotary must identify clearly its image and purpose to the general public, as well as to prospective and current members.

Another feature is for Rotary Clubs to select, on a voluntary basis, a "matched club," or partner club in another part of the world. Over a period of years, these friendship experiences would involve joint projects, volunteer service, exchange programs, club visitations and other goodwill relationships to enhance club service activities and build new levels of international understanding.

The Committee also appeals to the Rotary world to accept that Rotary is truly a dual gender organization. This is a dream to be achieved now — not just some day in the future. Women Rotarians deserve the dignity and respect afforded to all club members. All Rotarians must have the same opportunities for growth, leadership opportunities and recognition within the Rotary organization.

All of the dreams for The Rotary Foundation are limited only by the funds contributed annually. To make dreams come true, the Committee urges that a policy be adopted to encourage every Rotarian to make a voluntary contribution each and every year to The Rotary Foundation, with a goal of total support to the Annual Programs Fund to reach US$100 million by the year 2005.

At the same time, the Permanent Fund endowment must grow and earn income to create new and expanded programs for the Foundation. It is the recommendation that Rotary establish a target of building the Permanent Fund to at least US$1 billion by he year 2025.

We are also proposing a five year action plan to concentrate our membership expansion to men and women under the age of 40 as a positive step to maintain Rotary International as a vigorous, energetic service organization. The time has come for Rotarians to reject the idea that a Rotary Club can only be a club of senior citizens, if we want to service for the next 100 years. It will require a serious commitment to restore youthful vigor to Rotary by emphasizing new membership under the age of 40.

Furthermore, we urge Rotarians to modify the language of Rotary so that young business and professional persons understand and accept the philosophy of Rotary. To younger generations who talk in the language of "networking, volunteerism, cyber communication and interfacing" our references to fellowship groups, fireside meetings and pathways to peace, may not be very attractive or relevant.

At the same time, we must revitalize traditional club meetings with new formats, creative programs, and discussions of relevant issues. This will require more effective training methods for club leaders. We plan for clubs to change many of the "old-fashioned" formalities and procedures which create far too many dreary club meetings. Our very survival depends upon Rotary working for a new vitality and a greater relevancy as we more into the 21st Century.

Will anything happen to these dreams for the future? Only time will tell. But this we know...every new program and every new Rotary achievement starts with a single idea. Always remember, the most successful programs of Rotary began in one Rotary Club, with a dedicated group of leaders — not with the International Board of Directors or the President. I am convinced that the evolution of Rotary for its next hundred years was well beyond Paul Harris's wildest imagination, as is ours at this time.

Nearly 60 years ago, Paul Harris said at an International Convention, "Dreaming of the future of Rotary is not so bad, if you dream good dreams, and then make them come true." We have heard of some great dreams. It is now up to us, and those who follow us, to make them come true.

In my opinion, that's where Rotary will be going in the 21st Century!

14

DEDICATION

Webster defines it simply as "wholehearted devotion". Yet, it is the one ingredient most important for success in anything we do, whether it be in our family, our business or in everyday life.

Each of the vignettes you have read in this book was contributed by one of 35 dedicated Rotarians; as you can tell, they have found much pleasure and satisfaction from their membership in Rotary.

The word "dedicated" does not lend itself to superlatives, such as "more" or "most". But if it did, the most dedicated Rotarian whom I know and consider as the epitome of Rotary, is PDG Austin B. Watson of my own Rotary Club of Fair Park.

Austin was born in Dallas, Texas, one of eleven children whose father was a Baptist minister. At the age of 14, in 1928, Austin's older brother, Houston, got him a job with Westinghouse Electric Company. Both Austin and Houston worked for Westinghouse until 1947, when they both left to start their own company, Watson Electric Supply Company in Dallas. When the family-owned company was sold 50 years later, it had 20 branches throughout East, Central and South Texas.

He and his lovely "bride", Millie, have recently celebrated their 65th wedding anniversay. Believe me, that takes *dedication*, too.

Austin joined the Rotary Club of Fair Park in 1951, shortly after it was chartered. He served as president of the club in 1954-1955. That was the year when Herbert J. Taylor, the author of Rotary's 4-Way Test, became president of Rotary International. Thirteen years later, Austin became Governor of Rotary District 581. It was during that year that he met and became well acquainted with Herbert Taylor, visiting he and his wife, Gloria, on a number of occasions. The 4-Way Test, which follows this chapter, cite the personal and business principles that Austin has lived by.

His time, his thoughts, and his energy have always been directed toward serving others. While I was district chairman of International Youth Exchange, he would not let me rest until I had invited all foreign exchange students from thoughout the district to be his guest for dinner at the private club to which he belonged. And like the Jewish mother, ("eat, eat"), he insisted that everyone have pie alamode. This same invitation has been extended to every Group Study Exchange team that our club has hosted for the past 20 years. During 1972, I became involved with a Rotary project to refurbish a ward at the State Hospital in Terrell. When he saw the plans, he said, "I want to furnish all of the light fixtures...and I'll send out an electrician to install them."

Those people who know Austin understand when I refer to him as a "silent philanthropist", contributing to so very many charities and causes, and asking not to be recognized. His favorite charity is the world-famous Texas Scottish Rite Hospital for Children, on whose Board he has served since 1982 and is presently one of the Vice-Presidents.

Austin has been the editor of Fair Park's weekly newsletter, "Rotanews" since 1954. During those 45 years, he has never missed an issue. Now, *that's dedication!* It is mailed to over 200 Rotarians each week. During the years that the club has offered to re-imburse him for postage, he has always sent the check back with the request that it be sent to the Rotary Foundation. He is a multiple Paul Harris Fellow (many times over) with 47 years perfect attendance.

It is with great pleasure and admiration
that I dedicate this Rotary book to
PDG Austin B. Watson

THE ROTARY INTERNATIONAL THEME 1992-93

Real Happiness is Helping Others

NOTES

NOTES

THE 4-WAY TEST

of the things we think, say or do

First: Is it the truth?

Second: Is it fair to all concerned?

Third: Will it build goodwill and better friendships?

Fourth: Will it be beneficial to all concerned?